Jossey-Bass Teacher

Jossey-Bass Teacher provides K–12 teachers with essential knowledge and tools to create a positive and lifelong impact on student learning. Trusted and experienced educational mentors offer practical classroom-tested and theory-based teaching resources for improving teaching practice in a broad range of grade levels and subject areas. From one educator to another, we want to be your first source to make every day your best day in teaching. *Jossey-Bass Teacher* resources serve two types of informational needs—essential knowledge and essential tools.

Essential knowledge resources provide the foundation, strategies, and methods from which teachers may design curriculum and instruction to challenge and excite their students. Connecting theory to practice, essential knowledge books rely on a solid research base and time-tested methods, offering the best ideas and guidance from many of the most experienced and well-respected experts in the field.

Essential tools save teachers time and effort by offering proven, ready-to-use materials for in-class use. Our publications include activities, assessments, exercises, instruments, games, ready reference, and more. They enhance an entire course of study, a weekly lesson, or a daily plan. These essential tools provide insightful, practical, and comprehensive materials on topics that matter most to K–12 teachers.

D1297981

The Substitute Teaching Survival Guide, Grades 6–12

Emergency Lesson Plans and Essential Advice

John Dellinger

JOSSEY-BASS
A Wiley Imprint
www.josseybass.com

Published by Jossey-Bass
A Wiley Imprint
989 Market Street, San Francisco, CA 94103-1741   www.josseybass.com

Jossey-Bass books and products are available through most bookstores. To contact Jossey-Bass directly call our Customer Care Department within the U.S. at 800-956-7739, outside the U.S. at 317-572-3986, or fax 317-572-4002.

Jossey-Bass also publishes its books in a variety of electronic formats. Some content that appears in print may not be available in electronic books.

ISBN 0-7879-7411-0

Printed in the United States of America
FIRST EDITION
PB Printing   10 9 8 7 6 5 4 3 2 1

About the Book

When teachers are absent from their classrooms, substitute teachers are often left with no directions, no lesson plans, and no way to control the kids. How can a substitute teacher maintain order in the classroom, much less engage the students in a meaningful learning experience?

While most books for substitute teachers offer tips and suggestions for classroom management, this unique volume also provides an even more important resource: over sixty-seven ready-to-use emergency lesson plans for language arts, mathematics, social studies, and science for grades 6 through 12. With 152 useful suggestions and a daily outline of activities, complete with checklists, this book is an essential tool for both the novice and the experienced substitute teacher for grades 6 through 12. A perfect resource for substitute teachers themselves as well as regular classroom teachers who wish to plan ahead for their absence, this book will allow substitute teachers of all levels to quickly acquire key information that will make the difference between a good day of teaching and a complete disaster.

The Author

John Dellinger taught in the public school systems of Riverside, California; Boulder, Colorado; Steamboat Springs, Colorado; and Denver, Colorado. After retiring from the Denver Public Schools, he continued to teach as a substitute in Denver and neighboring Jefferson County.

He is the author of two detective/mystery novels, *Dinosaur Tracks & Murder* and *Homecoming to Murder,* published as audio books by Books in Motion. He has had articles published in the following magazines: *Vietnam, Grit, Wild West, Adventure West, World War II, Military History, Short Stuff, Historically JeffCo, The Retired Officer, Rocky Mountain Rider, Great Battles,* and as a part of "Soundings" in *Air & Space/Smithsonian.*

He holds degrees from two universities: a B.A. from the University of Northern Colorado and an M.A. from the University of Colorado.

Contents

This book is dedicated to America's teachers, whose job sometimes seems impossible, but they get it done.

Preface

This book contains valuable information for both substitute teachers and regular teachers. Successful substitute teaching is a partnership agreement between the substitute and the regular teacher that results in a productive day of student learning when the regular teacher is absent from the classroom. This book offers suggestions on how to achieve that productive day of student learning.

The word "suggestions" is used because I am not foolish enough to think all teachers will agree with everything that is written in this book. It is rare for teachers to totally agree on anything, but it is hoped that there will be enough agreement that teachers, substitute and regular, will find this book a valuable resource that aids them in the all-important task of educating students.

This book is a product of the many years I spent teaching in public schools. I taught middle school and high school, social studies and English. During the course of my teaching career I taught in four different school districts and in six different schools. After retiring from the Denver Public Schools, I substituted in Denver and in neighboring Jefferson County. Most of the things, perhaps all of the things, I write about are based on personal experiences.

In the book I have not recounted my personal experiences, since I do not wish to burden you with reminiscences that are probably similar to those of most retired teachers. Besides, you are building your own reminiscences, and those are the nuggets of experience that are the most meaningful to you. I can only point out what I think are strategies that will help you achieve teaching success. I extend to every teacher, regular and substitute, my best wishes for a pleasant and successful time in the classroom.

John Dellinger

Chapter One

The Role of the Substitute Teacher

Every school day a vast corps of substitute teachers marches into the nation's schools. Separated by school districts and states as varied as Alaska and Arizona, they are, nevertheless, a part of a vigilant network of dedicated professionals who keep the education of America's children from being interrupted. Rarely recognized for their contributions to education, usually underappreciated, often underpaid, mostly ignored and forgotten in discussions of education, substitute teachers are vital to the functioning of America's schools.

School superintendents can be absent from their jobs for a lengthy time, and schools continue to operate. Principals and other members of the administrative staff, as well as support staff, can attend meetings, conferences, or whatever, and usually their absences have little, if any, impact on what goes on inside classrooms. The absence that does not go unnoticed is the absence of the classroom teacher.

If a teacher steps out of the classroom for even five minutes, the classroom atmosphere changes. Maybe it is just a seventh-grade boy who throws a spit wad he has been waiting to throw all morning. Maybe it is the sophomore girl who leans forward to tell her friend about the telephone conversation she had last night. Maybe it is the third-grade boy who leans forward and uses his forefinger to flick the earlobe of the girl in front of him, causing her to look up from the book she is reading. Subtle changes in classroom learning that start out as a trickle become a torrent if the teacher is not nearby to stop the flow.

When a teacher is gone for an entire class period, a day, or longer, it is obvious that someone must fill in for him or her. Director of learning, keeper of the peace, mentor, substitute parent, evaluator of learning, counselor, friend, role model—the list goes on and on of what a teacher is to students. A teacher is too important to not have someone attempt to do the job that needs to be done to keep students on the path of learning while the teacher is gone.

The word "substitute" carries within it the meaning of "temporary." The role of a substitute teacher is not to alter, change, rearrange, innovate, deprecate, but, as nearly as possible, to duplicate the regular teacher. At times, one of the most difficult tasks a substitute has is to follow the pattern set by the regular teacher when the substitute disagrees with that pattern.

Teachers are as varied as what they put up on the bulletin boards and walls of their class-rooms. One teacher may run a free-wheeling, seemingly out-of-control zoo. Another teacher may be as rigid as a straight-back wooden chair.

A substitute often is plunked down in a classroom without having any advance knowledge of what the teacher and students are like. Add to this unknown the basic personality, teaching skill level, experience, mental alertness, and disposition of the substitute teacher on a particular day, the mix is very interesting—sometimes even volatile.

Although a substitute's role is to duplicate as best he or she can the role of the regular teacher in the classroom, it is an impossible task. Teachers who expect a substitute to function exactly as they would are in for a disappointment. Substitutes who expect to come in on a temporary basis and perform exactly as the regular teacher would are fooling themselves. Until cloning of teachers becomes the way of creating a substitute pool, expectations of being an exact replacement for a teacher are inflated.

Indeed, there are times when neither the regular teacher nor the substitute should expect the substitute to carry out an assignment in the same manner as the regular teacher. The regular teacher may have tremendous success in letting kids break into groups, with some of the kids in various places in the hall, the school library, or a computer room and part of the group in the classroom. A substitute who does not know the kids may not adequately be able to monitor student behavior in such a scenario.

When a regular teacher has left a lesson plan that a substitute determines cannot be executed as instructed, the substitute should alter the plan accordingly. If the lesson plan is beyond repair, he or she may wish to turn to the back of the book and choose an appropriate plan that will get him or her through the class with a minimum of difficulty.

Sometimes students will make requests that the regular teacher may or may not let them do:

STUDENT: "Mr. Glover lets us go to the library if we want to. I'm going to the library." (Possible translation: "I don't want to be in class and I am going to hang out with my friends in the high school cafeteria.")

SUBSTITUTE: "Mr. Glover may let you do that because he is your regular teacher. I'm sorry, but as a substitute I can't do that. School rules are that I'm supposed to keep you in class." (Possible translation: "I'm not going to risk you going someplace and getting in trouble—and getting me in trouble. Sit down and do your work like everyone else.")

Differentiating yourself from the regular teacher can be beneficial in many situations. Although you are trying to duplicate the learning experience the students would normally have, point out the difference between a substitute and the regular teacher when it is to your advantage in maintaining control or instituting the lesson plan. "You say Ms. Jackson lets you sit anyplace and doesn't follow her seating chart. I'm sorry, but as a substitute I don't know your names. Ms. Jackson left me this seating chart to help me know you. When she comes back, it is between you and her where you sit. For today, we are going to follow the chart because that's the way Ms. Jackson wants it."

Sometimes a substitute may find himself or herself in a completely untenable situation, either because of the lesson plan (or lack of one) or because of the way the regular teacher runs the classroom. When a regular teacher has totally lost control of a group of kids or is in a constant state of war with a class, it is very difficult for a substitute to come in on a one-day basis and put the education train back on track. If the regular teacher is so "laid back" that there is almost no structure to the class, how is a substitute to have enough authority to get the kids on task, if there is a task?

When a substitute is faced with an untenable situation, the substitute has three choices:

1. Ride it out the best he or she can, using innovation, creativity, and anything he or she might think of on the spur of the moment to give structure to the immediate situation. In such cases, a substitute has to be careful that the innovation at the spur of the moment doesn't blow up in the substitute's face. Chapter Two gives tips on getting a difficult class under control.

2. Call for help from another faculty member (the teacher next door, the team teacher, the department chair, a counselor, a school administrator, or whoever might be listed as being a person to whom you can turn for help). Many schools issue a substitute folder at the beginning of the day with pertinent information that includes who can be of help.

3. "Walk." (I recommend that you call the office and tell somebody you are leaving the classroom before you leave. If possible, wait for somebody to relieve you. Having somebody relieve you could become important because legal consequences could result from your departure.) Is "walking" a good step to take? Usually not, but you are better off leaving the classroom if you are in an abusive or out-of-control situation than staying and putting up with it. If you remain, you risk having the situation deteriorate further, possibly subjecting yourself to physical harm or liability for what may happen to someone in the class. You also risk losing your composure (temper, "cool") and verbally or physically assaulting a class or student. Besides, you are not paid enough to become either a verbal or physical punching bag for any student or class.

Sometimes, it is extremely difficult, but a substitute must maintain a professional demeanor at all times. When a substitute cannot maintain a professional demeanor, the substitute needs to "walk." The failure is not that of the substitute, but the failure of the school administration and the regular teacher to maintain a classroom where a substitute can function as a temporary replacement.

In functioning as a temporary replacement, the substitute needs to realize that kids have built a bond of trust, expectations, love (or hate), dependence, mutual interest, and companionship with the regular teacher. Kids do not have the same level of commitment to a substitute. It cannot be achieved in one day. If the substitute substitutes frequently with the same group of kids (often just being in the same school frequently), the kids and the substitute build their own bond.

"Hi, Ms. Bird. Who are you substituting for?"

"I'm doing Mr. Waters's class today."

"Too bad. I wish it was us."

Teachers are sometimes quick to pass judgment on a substitute: "I had a terrible substitute; the kids only completed about half of what I wanted done, and none of it was done right." Could it be that the teacher left a terrible lesson plan or that the kids were little devils that day?

Regular teachers have to remember that it is not an easy job to take over a class on a temporary basis. The students and situation are not familiar to the substitute; neither are the students familiar with the substitute. It is somewhat akin to a pilot stepping into the cockpit of an airplane and flying to a chartered destination where the pilot has never flown before. A competent pilot will usually get the job done, but the passengers may experience some air turbulence along the way, or possibly even end up at the wrong airport.

Substitute teachers have to remember that it is not an easy job to shepherd students through a semester or an entire year. Isn't it the truth that the little lambs (or ferocious beasts) are always looking for an opportunity to go astray? Keeping their wayward natures on the learning path day after day can wear down even the strongest of teachers. Yes, the substitute may have had to put up with a tough group of students for one day. Think how tough it is for a regular teacher who has to face them every day.

Don't be quick to pass judgment on a teacher or school. That is not why you are there. You have not been called in as an educational expert to rectify the wrongs of the regular teacher. You are there to carry on the pattern of education that has been set by the regular teacher.

Although there is no written law against it, it is bad form for a substitute to criticize a teacher to others. You may leave your substitute day thinking that Mr. Delbert is the worst teacher in the universe. Bad as you think he is, don't broadcast it to the whole universe. Bear your scorn in silence—be professional—just don't substitute for him again. If he is as bad as you think he is, others who have the authority to do so will take corrective measures.

If you are an experienced teacher who substitutes or a substitute who has substituted for a long time, you may be reluctant to follow a pattern that you know is not the best pattern for you. The regular teacher's lesson plan may call for you to work from an overhead projector and go line-by-line on an assignment. You may hate using an overhead and plodding along in lock-step fashion, preferring instead to rev up the kids with free-wheeling discussion as they absorb the main points the regular teacher wants them to learn. Do it the regular teacher's way, if possible. Unless it becomes largely impossible to follow the pattern set by the regular teacher, you are to do it his or her way, not yours.

You are not in a classroom to promote pet causes or theories. If your passion happens to be getting rid of the death penalty, saving wildlife, or whatever, your role is not to use the classroom as a platform for your personally held beliefs and causes. If you happen to believe that Edward de Vere wrote plays attributed to William Shakespeare and the teacher is teaching that Shakespeare wrote these plays, it is not your role to question what the teacher is teaching. Nor is it your role to promote AMWAY products or to put in a plug for your family's business. You are there to, as smoothly as possible, continue the learning that the regular teacher wants you to continue.

Occasionally, you may substitute for a teacher who is obviously using the classroom to promote his or her pet causes. For example, the classroom may be postered from one end to the other with anti-nuclear-power-plant material. The worksheet that you are supposed to go over with the kids may be totally one-sided.

In such a case, although the regular teacher expects you to be a minister of propaganda, you are a professional who is expected to educate rather than brainwash. Use the worksheet, but bring facts and some balance to the presentation. "Although a lot of people think that nuclear power plants are dangerous and should be banned, a lot of people think that they are safe enough that they need to be built because they cut down on the use of fossil fuels that emit some pollution. What do you think about that? Anybody have an opinion?" If worked properly, the class will provide balance to a one-sided presentation without you entering into the heart of the discussion.

As a substitute teacher, you are there to duplicate the regular teacher, but in so doing you should not sacrifice the greater goal of education, which is to present factual information to students, from which they can be spurred into inquiry, from which they can think and reach conclusions. In attempting to duplicate the regular teacher, you are not a clone and you are not there to turn students into clones.

Chapter One Summary of Suggestions

1. Try to duplicate the regular teacher as much as possible, but realize that it is impossible to be an exact replacement for the regular teacher.

2. As a regular teacher, don't expect a substitute to be an exact replacement for you.

3. Under most circumstances, try to follow the lesson plan that the regular teacher has left.

4. A substitute should alter a lesson plan if it is apparent that to try to carry it out is bad judgment.

5. Differentiate yourself from the regular teacher when it is to your benefit.

6. When faced with an untenable situation, try to ride it out, call for help, or leave the classroom ("walk").

7. If you are trying to ride out a bad situation by using innovation, creativity, or something you come up with on the spur of the moment, be aware that the situation can quickly deteriorate even further.

8. If you decide to "walk," call the office and let somebody know that you are leaving.

9. If "walking," wait for somebody to relieve you, if possible.

10. Maintain a professional demeanor at all times.

11. If a situation is so bad that you cannot maintain a professional demeanor, "walk."

12. Realize that students have a stronger bond and commitment to the regular teacher than you can build in a short time as a substitute.

13. Regular teachers should not be quick in passing judgment on substitutes.

14. Substitute teachers should not be quick in passing judgment on regular teachers.

15. Regular teachers have to remember that substitutes do not have an easy job.

16. Substitutes have to remember that regular teachers do not have an easy job.

17. Remember that you have not been called in as a substitute to pass judgment on a teacher or a school.

18. Don't tell others that you think a particular teacher is a terrible teacher; just don't substitute for that teacher again.

19. Even when you disagree with how the regular teacher wants you to do something, you should do it the regular teacher's way, if possible.

20. Do not use the classroom to promote pet causes.

21. If a regular teacher expects you to be a minister of propaganda, try to bring a factual balance to what it is the regular teacher wants you to present.

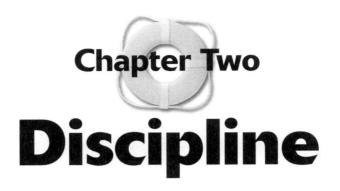

Chapter Two

Discipline

Discipline begins long before the substitute enters the classroom. Discipline (control of students, behavioral management of students, whatever you want to call it) is rooted in history, the society, the family, and many forces outside of the school that have produced the expectations of behavior that influence a student's actions when he or she is at school. Does a Japanese student say to a teacher in Japanese the equivalent of "Hey bro, what's up?"

Of more immediate concern to the substitute is the particular school at which you are substituting. Most schools have in place rules and discipline procedures that aid the substitute in performing his or her job. A substitute folder is usually given to the substitute by one of the school secretaries when the substitute checks in. A good substitute folder will help you by giving you the following:

1. The time schedule of classes for that day.

2. The class schedule and room or room numbers of the teacher for whom you are substituting.

3. Where the teacher's lesson plan is located (on desk, in teacher's desk drawer, in office box, or wherever). If you can't find the lesson plan, call the office for help. If there is still no lesson plan, use an emergency lesson plan from this book.

4. The name or names a substitute is to call if in need of help.

5. Referral forms, which are often included in the sub folder if that is how the school handles discipline problems, with instructions on how to refer a student.

6. A school map, with faculty restrooms and faculty lounges clearly marked (very helpful in a large school).

When you have found the classroom and have the lesson plan that you are going to use, how do you take control of the class? If you have time before class, locate seating charts and study the lesson plan. Of some help in establishing your authority and avoiding the questions "Are you a substitute?" and "Is Ms. Garfunkel out today?" is to write the date on the board and the words: "Ms. Garfunkel is out today. Thanks for your cooperation. Mr. Pelver."

That tells the kids that Ms. Garfunkel is gone; that you are the substitute; what your name is; and puts a mild note of friendliness into the situation, with an inference that you expect them to cooperate. Depending on the specific situation, the words "Sit in your assigned seats, please," might be added. This would more often be used with middle school students than elementary and high school students, since middle school students are more likely to challenge the established order of things.

Classroom discipline is akin to the "accordion paragraphs" middle school curriculums often require students to learn. Elementary school starts with nurturing and socializing the child, with the restrictions and rules teachers feel are necessary. By the time students are in middle school, tight discipline is usually required. Middle school students will quickly fall apart if a teacher does not have firm rules in place. As students advance into the upper grades of high school, restrictions and rules can be relaxed somewhat. High school freshmen, particularly at the beginning of the school year, may need a great deal of structure to restrict inappropriate behavior. High school seniors still require some direction, but it is usually minimal unless the regular teacher has let the class get so far out of control that rigid rules must be instituted to restore proper behavior.

Thus, in using the accordion analogy, fewer disciplinary measures are required in the beginning years of the education process, more discipline is required in the middle years, and discipline recedes in the advanced grade levels. A kindergarten or first-grade teacher might disagree with this as the teacher struggles to get the students into a learning structure. A high school teacher might disagree with the idea that seniors need less discipline when they have "senioritus" and can only think about getting out of school. It is unlikely that a middle school teacher would disagree that middle school kids require the most structure and are the greatest challenge to keep from overrunning the bounds of educational decency.

All students, whether elementary, middle, or high school, should be made aware by the regular teacher that they are to treat a substitute with the proper respect. They should also be made aware that if a substitute turns in the name of a student to the regular teacher for misbehavior, the student is in trouble and a consequence will follow.

Some teachers do not realize the importance to a substitute of a seating chart. The substitute doesn't know the kids. Without a seating chart, a substitute is flying blindly. It is very important, particularly in middle school, for a substitute to be able to identify each student and to have each student in a particular place in the classroom.

A regular teacher's notation to a substitute "I let the kids sit anyplace. They are good kids." is usually a recipe for substitute disaster. The substitute has no way to reach out and verbally take control of a student. Sometimes the substitute, without the seating chart, cannot even take attendance accurately. "You there, be quiet." doesn't cut it. "Charles, you are making too much noise. You need to be quiet so that we can hear Melissa read." Specific identification often does cut it, particularly when the regular teacher requires kids to be accountable for their behavior.

A substitute may have a terrific day with a cooperative class of juniors and seniors without a seating chart. It depends on the maturity level and the cooperation level of the class. Some classes, such as drama, debate, choir, etc., may never use a seating chart and may never require one for a substitute. Regular teachers, when realizing how important a seating chart is to a substitute in most classes, know their classes well enough to know whether or not the class requires a seating chart for a substitute. Regular teachers should not leave a substitute hanging by not having a seating chart when one should be left.

A seating chart left on a computer is not a good seating chart for a substitute. A substitute should not be tied to a computer for identifying kids. A substitute may move from place to place in the room as he or she presents a lesson. Running back to the computer by the teacher's desk every couple of minutes to identify the student the substitute calls on is not a good way to teach the class.

Writing on the board can also be valuable in maintaining classroom discipline. Some teachers don't leave a substitute any space to write on the board in the front of the room. Substitutes should never be confronted with a board that is totally filled and has the word "Save" on it. Where is a substitute to write things that may need to be written? Sometimes, particularly for elementary school and middle school, a student's name written on the board can do wonders in corrective behavior. For high school students, particularly sophomore and above, it is less necessary and not as effective.

For middle school and lower grades, and sometimes even high school freshmen, a substitute might write the following on the board and leave the results for the regular teacher:

Class Rating:

Period 1

Period 2

Period 3

Period 4

Period 5

Period 6

Disruptive Students (if any)

You may tell students at the beginning of the class that they will receive a class rating at the end of the class. Rate each class one of the following: Excellent, Very Good, Good, Fair, Bad. Put any disruptive student's name on the board. After a reasonable time of the student being non-disruptive, erase the name. You, the substitute, are in control. This is a way to reach out to the student and, without saying or doing anything other than writing his or her name on the board, telling the student, "Hey, kid, I'm in charge here. You need to behave yourself or your name gets turned in as disruptive." If the regular teacher has any kind of control over the student, the technique will usually be effective.

In a particularly good class, with only a name or two on the board, a disruptive student can often be persuaded into good behavior by saying something like, "You know, Josh, you are going to feel pretty silly if your name is the only name I have to turn in to Ms. Billings. Don't you think it would be a good idea to get your name off the board?"

Sometimes it may be a good technique to put the rating chart up on the board later in the class, rather than at the beginning. If you thought there would be no need for a rating chart or writing names on the board, but the behavior of the class has degenerated, it is not too late to put names on the board and/or use a rating chart. "Ladies and gentlemen, your behavior seems to be getting a little out of control; therefore, I'm going to give your class a rating of excellent, very good, good, fair, or bad. The rating will be turned in to your regular teacher, along with the names of troublemakers. Ms. Conway won't be very happy with you if you get a rating she doesn't like."

In some classes, no amount of putting names on the board and class ratings will make much difference. These are the kids who have little or no respect for a substitute or perhaps any form of authority.

A technique worth trying, under some circumstances, is a "good list." "O.K., ladies and gentlemen, I'm making my good list. If you want to be on it, you need to be doing your work and staying out of trouble. When I think you fit that description, I'll bring you my good list and have you sign it. That way Mr. Filbert will know who worked and who just played around. If you get on my good list, don't get knocked off it by bad behavior."

When kids see other kids getting signed up on the good list, they start feeling left out. Being a part of a good group can be just as great an incentive as not being part of a bad group.

In general, what should be the substitute's attitude toward maintaining classroom discipline? Does a substitute need to come into a classroom and assume the role of a Marine drill instructor? Should a substitute come in as meek as a repentant child? Hard-nosed, namby-pamby, or somewhere in the middle?

Start out pleasantly, if possible. Don't expect defiance where there may be none. If the room is in complete chaos, with students possibly even unwilling to sit down, your voice or the board at the front of the room may be all that you have at your disposal. It depends on the situation, but a notation on the board may bring results: "If you do not sit down and be quiet, I will be forced to call the office."

Unfortunately for you and the students, when a class starts out badly, you have lost the most valuable thing a substitute can have—cooperation of the students. Assume the students will be cooperative. Be firm, if necessary, but start the class on a cooperative note. "Good morning, ladies and gentlemen. As you can see, I'm not Ms. Hardwit. Let's take roll and then we'll get into what Ms. Hardwit expects us to do today."

Calling the students "ladies and gentlemen," even if they are not, often has a soothing effect on their behavior. It establishes a standard of expectations without them even being aware of it. "The sub treated us with respect. Usually I'm the biggest mess-off in class. The sub doesn't know that. Maybe I'll be good today."

Middle school students may require a very firm hand at the beginning of class. Try the easygoing approach first, but quickly switch to hard-line if necessary. Middle school students, as well as high school freshmen, can quickly push the limits if you let them. Your job is to not let them push you into being a non-authority figure.

Sometimes, attendance-taking is delayed, depending on how the teacher has structured the class and whatever it is you have to teach on a particular day. Many schools will want the attendance office to have a list of your absentees within the first twenty minutes of the period. In general, it is best to get the students into an assigned seat and get them in a working mode by taking attendance at the start of the class. Doing this has the psychological effect of "Passing period is over. I'm in class. My attitude and behavior are different from when I'm not in class."

Passing periods are usually anywhere from five to ten minutes. Some high schools have passing periods of ten minutes. Some middle schools have passing periods as short as three minutes. The length of the passing period may alter how soon into the class period you take roll. Three-minute passing periods (particularly barbaric for a substitute who is substituting for a teacher who has five classes in a row—yes, it does happen, not often, but substitutes have been in such circumstances)—can cause a delay in roll taking, unless you want to take it several times when kids who have been shoving their way through crowded halls dribble in at various times.

Now that the class has started (one hopes, with cooperation and good will, or at least with no noticeable discipline problems), maintain the pleasantness and cooperation, if possible. You may have to get very disagreeable before the class is over, but it is very possible that the cooperation and good will may spread throughout the period and you will end the class thinking what good kids they are. Initially, you are setting a tone of cooperative behavior. If you can keep that same tone, both you and your day and the students' day will be better. Modify your behavior and attitude toward the class if it becomes necessary to modify their behavior.

A regular classroom teacher, who is going to be with the kids throughout the year, may have to start out the year "laying down the law," particularly with middle school students. Much of this depends on the individual teacher's personality and the way the teacher interacts with students. Whatever the case, it is establishing a long-term relationship, with the teacher setting the rules and standards he or she expects students to follow.

When a substitute arrives, the rules and standards of the class have already been set by the regular teacher. The substitute must fit into the class for only one day (perhaps longer). If possible, gain the cooperation of the class by a pleasant attitude and demeanor at the beginning of the class. The class may become uncooperative, but don't make it happen by starting out with the attitude "As a substitute, these kids are going to run all over me if I don't lay down the law right away. I've got to be tough as nails or they are going to chew me up like dog meat."

Conversely, a substitute can't have the attitude "Anything goes," or it will. You are the authority figure in the class. Apply your authority gently, but firmly. "You two gentlemen, in the back. This is a test. Ms. Garcia said that I was not to let you talk or help each other. These are the instructions she left me. That is the way we are doing it. No more talking or I've got to pick up your test and you get zeros."

Substitutes should be aware of the mind-set of today's students. In previous generations, teachers may have barked and students jumped. Not anymore. American society and schools have created a student who expects approval and very little disapproval. Rights, not responsibilities, are where the emphasis is placed. Self-fulfillment and positive reinforcement are expected by today's students. Regular teachers are sometimes viewed as "buddies" more than authority figures. Whether this is good or bad, it doesn't matter to the substitute; the reality is that the substitute has to deal with it.

While regular teachers are expected to hold the line on discipline all year, a substitute usually only holds it for one day. A substitute can have a miserable day trying to enforce standards and discipline that may not be the norm in a particular class. A substitute can have a very good day merely trying to hold the students within the bounds of acceptable behavior, working within what appear to be the rules and standards of the regular teacher. If the regular teacher lets kids flop down on the floor while watching a video, the substitute has to decide whether or not it is worth the fight to make kids sit at their desks or tables.

Some things are unacceptable, no matter how permissive the regular teacher. A few examples: Don't let kids throw books out the window; don't let the "little dears" destroy the room; don't let students mutilate other students. Setting fires, smoking, drinking alcohol, engaging in sexual activity, and calling you names are things you should not allow.

A common occurrence is students wanting to leave the classroom. Let your rule be "valid passes for valid reasons." Only grant permission to go someplace when the student can present you with a pass or give you a reason that justifies your issuing the student a pass. You will eliminate many headaches for yourself by only permitting one student at a time to be out of the class to use the bathroom, unless unusual circumstances warrant otherwise.

Discipline outside of the classroom should not be a substitute's major concern. You may have to stand duty in place of the regular teacher, but don't let it become a situation that is threatening to you or to a student.

A pleasant manner can be your greatest asset on hall duty or some other form of supervision duty that you are required to perform.

"Hi, ladies, do you have a pass?"

"We don't need a pass."

"I'm sorry, but I can't let you go this way without a pass."

"Who says so?"

"The school says so, and I'm just following what they tell me to do on hall duty. Show me a pass and I'll be glad to let you go this way."

If the kids walk by you and continue to go where they are not supposed to go, don't physically restrain them. After a non-threatening request to return, don't turn the situation into a verbal confrontation. Let them go while you seek help from a regular faculty member, an administrator, or any authority figure who happens to be nearby. As a substitute, do the best you can, but don't get into major confrontations with students. If no one is nearby, you have done what you can do, other than perhaps reporting it.

In some cases, if you report it to an administrator or a counselor, he or she won't want to hear it. You will be viewed as a disruption to the day, an outsider who is creating a problem he or she doesn't want to deal with. It depends on the school and the personnel involved. Some schools are on top of everything and administrators appreciate being informed of violations of school rules, while others are less attentive to the concerns of substitutes.

As a substitute, carry out a supervision situation so that when it is over, you have done what can be reasonably expected. If asked by an administrator or faculty member, "Why are kids down that hall?" reply, "I asked them for passes and told them to stop, but they kept going." Honestly recount what happened and let those who have the authority to deal with students do so.

As a substitute, you are a professional. Professional judgment is expected and should be exercised by you. In this day of bomb threats, school shootings, and other forms of societal deviancy, you should be alert to potential dangers in school. In a supervision situation, report any abnormal behavior to school authorities. Maybe the kid is only carrying a jagged piece of metal to metal shop for a class project, or could it be a lethal weapon? If you let somebody know, you have done your duty.

At times, as a substitute, you will be placed in a difficult supervision assignment. Lunchroom duty, playground supervision, taking kids to an assembly where they are supposed to sit in assigned seats and you are supposed to keep them quiet during the performance, an activity where they are milling around in a semi-dark gymnasium with loud music blasting in your ears (worthy of workman's compensation when you can prove hearing loss)—these supervision assignments can be benign or deadly; it depends. Your job again, do what can be reasonably expected. If something goes awry because of the situation, the fault is not yours, but that of those who structured the situation and put you in it.

On supervision assignments (such as lunchroom duty) where there may be other teachers serving duty with you, defer to the regular teachers. Follow their lead or instructions, but don't expect to be the same authority figure as any of them may be. If you have asked a kid to pick up the empty milk carton he threw on the floor and he doesn't do it, don't get into a verbally escalating situation. Get help from the other supervising teacher if there is one. If not, it may be advisable to back off and leave it be. Another approach that some feel is beneath their dignity is to pick it up yourself with an instructive comment such as, "It makes a lot nicer lunch room if we keep it cleaned up."

In some supervising situations, the kids themselves can be of great help. Leading students in from the playground to the cafeteria, taking kids to the library, taking kids someplace when you don't know where it is, monitoring students in a computer lab, the kids usually know what is expected of them. They will usually help you if you have established a spirit of cooperation. Some kids take advantage of the situation, but there is usually a large corps of students who will let you know what is expected of students in a particular situation. Leaving the regular teacher the names of the particularly helpful students can reinforce the idea that good behavior has its rewards.

Sometimes, there is nothing for a substitute to do but ride out a bad situation. Advisement periods and activity periods are something that counselors, administrators, and those who don't have to monitor them seem to particularly like. Regular teachers and substitutes, who have a room full of screaming kids with nothing to do but play games or whatever, may have a different opinion of the worth of an advisement or activity period.

The substitute, when involved in such a situation, needs to relax and follow whatever procedures the regular teacher has in place. So what if some kids are shooting dice in the corner of the room while others are lying on bean bags and watching others shoot paper wads into the wastebasket? If that is what normally goes on, let it roll, unless it gets too far out of control. Curbing usual activities can be a real hassle for a substitute. Again, do what can reasonably be expected, using good judgment in keeping kids from harming each other or destroying things.

All things pass, even a bad class period. As a substitute, you will feel much better if you keep your blood pressure under control.

Whatever the class or supervision assignment, be calm and do what can reasonably be expected. It is not your task to come in like a Western frontier marshal and corral the varmints. You are just maintaining the peace on a one-day basis. Do it as low-key as possible, leaving the real town taming to the regular faculty and administrators.

One of the most important words in the English language for a substitute to remember is "RELAX." You are not being paid "combat pay," although at times you probably should be. At the end of the school day, go home with your blood pressure under control and your sanity intact.

To some, it may seem as if the advice given in this chapter is caving in to student pressure and not being enough of an authority figure. What reflects the reality of today does not reflect times past. We may or may not like it that teachers, with some individual exceptions, speak with less authority than in the past, but that is the case. Society is constantly changing, and perhaps teachers of the future will speak with more authority (or less). As a substitute, you have to function in current reality. Recognize the current reality, adjust to it, and have mostly good substitute days.

Chapter Two Summary of Suggestions

1. Schools should provide substitute folders to substitutes, containing:
   - The time schedule of classes for that day
   - The class schedule and room or room numbers of the teacher for whom the substitute is substituting

- Where the absent teacher's lesson plans are located
- Name or names and telephone numbers where the substitute can find help
- Referral forms and/or discipline procedures
- A school map with the faculty restrooms and faculty lounges clearly marked

2. Any instructions that a substitute is expected to read should be quickly decipherable and not overly long.

3. If you have time before class, locate seating charts and study the lesson plan.

4. You should write on the board, preferably even before the students come into class, that the regular teacher is out, thank the students for their expected cooperation, and sign your name.

5. In general, you should be the strictest in your discipline with middle school students, and less strict with elementary and high school students.

6. Regular teachers should inform and expect students to treat substitutes with respect; appropriate consequences should be instituted by the regular teacher when students do not behave properly for a substitute.

7. Regular teachers should, in most cases, leave an up-to-date seating chart for the substitute.

8. The seating chart should be one that the substitute can carry with him or her as he or she moves about the room.

9. Regular teachers should leave a substitute room to write on the board.

10. You may wish to rate a class on how well they behave and cooperate with you. A rating system of the following is suggested:
    - Excellent
    - Very Good
    - Good
    - Fair
    - Bad

Turn in the rating to the regular teacher.

11. Write the names of the disruptive students on the board. For those who continue to be disruptive, turn in their names to the regular teacher.

12. You may wish to make a "good list," leaving the regular teacher the names of students who were well-behaved and worked well.

13. Start the class with a positive, pleasant attitude, if possible.

14. For classes that won't settle down and give you their attention in a reasonable time, use your voice or write on the board that you will call the office if they don't sit down and become quiet.

15. Quickly switch to strict discipline with middle school students who are getting out of control.

16. Usually, it is best to get students into their seats and take attendance at the very beginning of class, but this may vary according to length of passing periods and other factors.

17. Set a tone of cooperation and good will at the beginning of the class, but modify your behavior and attitude toward the class if it becomes necessary to modify their behavior.

18. Don't have the attitude that you have to be tough as nails.

19. Don't have the attitude that anything goes.

20. Be aware that today's students are not as inclined to view teachers as authority figures as were some previous generations.

21. Realize that you are only holding the line on discipline for the length of your substituting assignment; it is the job of the regular teacher to set the standards and hold the line on discipline all year.

22. Hold students within the bounds of acceptable behavior, working within what appear to be the rules of the regular teacher.

23. Regardless of how permissive the regular teacher is, don't tolerate behavior that is obviously unacceptable.

24. Only permit students to leave the room with valid passes for valid reasons.

25. Only permit one student at a time to be out of the class to use the bathroom unless unusual circumstances warrant otherwise.

26. When on hall duty or some other supervision duty, have a pleasant manner.

27. Don't physically try to restrain students.

28. Don't get into verbal or physical confrontations with students.

29. On supervision assignments, seek help from an administrator or regular faculty member when needed.

30. On supervision assignments, do what can be reasonably expected.

31. On a supervision assignment, be alert to abnormal behavior that might indicate potential violence, and report it to school authorities.

32. When doing supervision assignments that are shared with regular teachers, follow the lead of regular teachers and seek their help when appropriate.

33. Use helpful students when appropriate.

34. When supervising students in an advisement or activity period, permit them to do what the regular teacher permits them to do, unless it is necessary to curb the activity as a matter of good judgment and maintaining control.

35. In all supervision assignments, be calm and maintain your composure.

36. Be aware of the current reality of education and adjust to it.

Chapter Three

Lesson Plans

The making of lesson plans is something over which a substitute has little control. The making of a lesson plan is the domain of the regular classroom teacher. The substitute is expected to carry out the lesson plan that he or she is given. Sometimes the plan is easy to follow; at other times, the plan is extremely difficult to execute.

The regular teacher should remember that the plan is not for the regular teacher, but for another person. The plan should be clear, concise, and have enough road marks, but not bog down in endless details that may confuse rather than aid the substitute. A well-made lesson plan left for a substitute is a partnership agreement that will benefit both the regular teacher and the substitute while fulfilling the ultimate objective of educating students.

A good lesson plan for the regular teacher is not always a good lesson plan for a substitute. For the regular teacher, who is totally familiar with the students, the subject matter, school procedures, and other school-related matters, the plan may be very easy to successfully implement. For a substitute, the same plan may be a swamp, ready to drag the substitute under the murky waters of classroom chaos.

What are the dos and don'ts of making good lesson plans and carrying them out? What kind of lesson plan is best for achieving maximum results for the partnership of regular teacher and substitute teacher?

Plans should be readily available and readable. Sometimes teachers jot down, scribble, scrawl, whatever, a set of blurred, poorly written instructions on whatever scrap of paper happens to be available. A student who handed in such a sloppy piece of work would be in danger of receiving an "F." The lesson plan doesn't have to be perfect, but it should be easy to read and able to convey quickly what the substitute is to do.

Some teachers will write the lesson plan on the board. That is fine, but what if a student, the school custodian, or someone else erases it? No lesson plan. "Help! What do I do now?" If a duplicate copy, written on paper, exists for the substitute, no problem. Writing a lesson plan or parts of a lesson plan on the board can be beneficial to a substitute, but only if a backup copy exists.

The same is true for plans that may be written on an overhead transparency and left on the overhead projector. What happens if that piece of plastic is lost or misplaced? What happens if a student comes in and slips that piece of plastic into a notebook and the sub never receives it and has no idea where it is? Is it possible that a student might intentionally smudge out what is on the transparency while the sub is taking attendance? In most cases, students are not out to destroy a lesson plan, but strange things can happen in a classroom.

Sub plans sent in by fax are also at risk of disappearing. What happens if the computer doesn't work, if the office doesn't give or send the plan to the substitute? Many things can go wrong or take up a sub's time in trying to locate the fax. No lesson plan and it's panic time for the substitute!

Then there is the teacher who says, "Call me at home and I'll give you the plans over the telephone." This creates multiple opportunities for misunderstanding what the teacher wants the substitute to do. A written set of plans, where the teacher has to sit down and write the plans, is far more reliable than plans that have been copied from a telephone conversation while the teacher is usually ad-libbing them.

Another lesson plan that can easily vanish is a lesson plan that depends totally on student participation. "Shawn and Michael will debate Jennifer and Melissa today. Don't worry; the kids will do it all. Just take roll and sit back and enjoy the debate. It will take all period."

What debate? Melissa was absent and Michael didn't feel like debating anyway. Jennifer said that Melissa had all of their debate notes and she couldn't debate without her. It's panic time for the substitute!

Student participation lesson plans are fine for a sub, as long as a backup plan exists. "If for some reason Shawn, Michael, Jennifer, and Melissa can't debate today, give out Worksheet 122. Have the students write their answers on the worksheets and collect them at the end of the period."

When a lesson plan is designed for student participation, it should not be overly complicated and should not overly involve the substitute. The regular teacher might be able to handle multiple tasks while having students participate in an activity, but a sub, who is trying to figure out a lesson plan, maintain discipline, and direct students in the activity, should not be required to take a major part in the activity.

Sometimes a substitute is given the instruction "Read the narration to the class as the kids read aloud the play." This unnecessarily constricts the sub's ability to control a class—the sub is expected to monitor the behavior of the class while having his or her nose tied to a book. For the regular teacher, who knows the kids and is familiar with the play, this is fine. For the sub, who is trying to stay with the play, Charlie may be talking to Joe in the third row while Susy, who has lost all interest in the play, is demanding a pass to the bathroom. The sub has to be able to monitor class behavior. Tying a sub to any particular task that keeps the sub from monitoring class behavior should not be a part of any lesson plan.

Sometimes a lesson plan will call for the substitute to grade students. "Give each student a participation grade. I usually give the students up to five points per day for participation. Mark the participation points in my grade book."

No! No! No! A substitute should never be required to enter a grade for a student. That is the responsibility of the regular teacher who has set the criteria for grading and knows the students. There are too many variables involved with the substitute doing the grading. "Ms. Lesser always gives me five points, even if I only say one thing. I deserve more than the two points you gave me." Having a class correct papers after an assignment is a different matter. "Ms. Boatright wants you to exchange papers as you usually do. She left me the answers and

I'll read them to you while you correct the papers." The sub is not overly constricted in reading the class answers and can still monitor the behavior of the class. The sub is not entering grades in a grade book; the sub merely collects the papers after the correcting is done.

There is only so much that a substitute can do in a period. The chief task of a substitute is to maintain order while instructing students on what they are to do. There is no time for a substitute to give grades, complete a checklist on each student, or engage in any activity that takes the substitute's focus away from ensuring that the classroom is an orderly place of learning.

The definition of "orderly place of learning" has in recent years come to embrace an even larger array of activities. Some might say that what students do, particularly in middle school, is "play games." For many teachers, the quiet concentration on a math problem or the "No talking; read the story by yourself." has become a full-blown activity with students doing everything but running up the walls. Good or bad? Opinions vary.

The regular teacher, who may do fine with a class doing "full-blown-games," should not expect the substitute to carry out such games with the same expertise. If you are a substitute who is faced with an overly complicated game or "wild activity," do the best that you can with it, but if you can't handle it, don't. You may have to modify it to keep the kids under control or completely shut it down if necessary. Hopefully, no teacher will expect you to grade such an activity.

Teachers' grade books are best not made available to a substitute. Grade books and attendance books are too precious to risk with a substitute, even when grades and attendance have been transferred to a computer. The substitute would not intentionally lose, misplace, or alter the grade book, but it could happen. Students have been known to take advantage of a regular teacher's absence to try to alter a grade book. Why risk it, when there is no need to risk it?

Substitutes should not grade; therefore, there is no need for a grade book. Substitutes should leave a list of absentees for the regular teacher, as well as submit absentee names to the attendance office, if so required. As long as a substitute has a class list (often a computer printout, supplied by the office) and a seating chart (supplied by the teacher), a substitute can perform the functions of "*non*-grading" and taking attendance.

Henry David Thoreau left to posterity the great cry "Simplify!" Henry lived in the woods and never faced a class of twenty-first-century students, but his nineteenth-century recommendation on life is very apropos to leaving lesson plans for a substitute.

Simplify—do not leave overly complex lesson plans for a substitute. The regular teacher has no need to impress the substitute with a brilliant lesson plan that shows the substitute how knowledgeable the regular teacher is. The substitute, who thinks that he or she is bored with just passing out a worksheet and having the kids do it, should remember that substituting is a job—you are not there to be entertained. Most subs will thank the regular teacher for leaving something that is easy to accomplish while permitting the sub time to monitor student behavior.

Teachers will sometimes leave a notation similar to the following: "You've got an easy day. Just show the video to all my classes." Easy day or not so easy day? It depends.

Most substitutes today are familiar with a variety of audiovisual equipment. Usually AV assignments go well, providing the equipment is available, works properly, the substitute knows how to operate it, and the class has been properly prepared for an AV assignment.

It is the responsibility of the regular teacher to see that the substitute doesn't have to run all over the building to get a VCR or some other piece of equipment. It is the responsibility of the regular teacher to have adequate assurance that the equipment will work properly before a lesson plan is left for a substitute involving the equipment. If the piece of equipment has peculiarities that may make it difficult to operate, instructions should be left for the substitute. "The VCR only works on channel 3 on both the TV and the VCR. Student announcements come in at the end of period 2 (9:33–9:38) on channel 58. You will need to switch the cord on the back and then re-switch it when the announcements are over. A number of students in the class know how to make the switch. Kevin, Carey, and Liz have been informed that they will be doing the switching for you."

For a regular teacher to prepare an AV assignment, sometimes it takes almost nothing, depending on the maturity level of the class and what it is the regular teacher wants to accomplish with the assignment. Some classes are relatively mature: "Have the students watch the last forty minutes of *Romeo and Juliet.* The video is set where you need to start. Sorry, but this VCR has no working 'counter' on it, so you will have to watch where you come in and then rewind to that point for the next class."

For some classes the regular teacher may leave something similar to the following: "Distribute the question sheets before you start the video. Make sure that the kids all sit in their assigned seats. Have the two students in the front corners move to the back seats in their rows, so that they can see the TV. Have students write answers on the question sheets during the video. Collect question sheets at the end of the video. Leave me the names of students who are not paying attention to the video."

A regular teacher should never "throw a video up in the air for a substitute"; in other words, a video is not for the purpose of allowing students to move by their friends, sit and talk, and socialize while absorbing nothing of the video. Videos should not be used for the purpose of killing a class period or giving the students a free period. Videos are instructional devices, and the regular teacher, when leaving plans for a substitute, should build into the plans for a substitute whatever it takes to ensure that the video is instructional.

As with any other assignment that can vanish, a backup assignment should be provided. "If something happens that you can't watch the video, have the students answer the questions on pages 95 through 98 of *Grammar for Today,* the red grammar books on the shelf in the back of the room. Collect work at the end of the period and check to see if we still have a total of thirty-three books on the shelf."

The regular teacher, in preparing a lesson plan, should not "overbook" or "underbook." It is difficult to know just how much time it will take to complete an assignment; usually, the more experienced the teacher is, the easier it is to judge how long a particular assignment will take students. If there is doubt, it is better to "overbook" than to "underbook."

A substitute who gives an assignment to students that only takes fifteen minutes in a forty-minute period is in trouble. On the other hand, there is no need for a lesson plan that lays out an hour and a half of work for a fifty-minute period and instructs the substitute to collect it at the end of the period, thinking that it will keep the kids so busy that they will not have time to get into trouble.

Why have the substitute collect work at all? Kids often do better for a substitute if they have an end-of-period deadline. If it is not due until the next day, the kids have a greater tendency to play around in class. "I'll do it at home tonight. I'd rather talk to Jamie now. I can't talk to her tonight, but I can do my work tonight."

A lesson plan that usually works well for a substitute has one part that takes up most of the period and then is collected at the end of the period. A second part of the assignment is open-ended and is not collected by the substitute: "Ms. Galviano wants you to get into your reading groups and read 'The Flight of the Dove.' The handout I am going to give you has seven questions on the end of it. You will have to answer them as a group, on a sheet of paper with all of your names at the top of the paper. Don't write on the handouts. When you have finished, turn in the paper and the handout. That part of the assignment is due today. After you have finished that, do this week's vocabulary assignment, which starts on page 202 of your vocabulary books. That is due at the beginning of the period tomorrow."

Long periods, particularly "block periods" of an hour and a half or so, may require more than one activity to keep the focus and interest of the class:

1. (30 minutes) Have the students watch the video "Birds of Brazil."

2. (30 minutes) After the video, have them write down descriptions for three of the birds. They choose the bird's and the description for each bird should be about a page (one-side).

3. (20 minutes) Have students read descriptions to the class, without using the names of the birds they are describing. Other students listen and write down three characteristics of each bird. When the class has correctly identified the bird, the students add the name of the bird to the three characteristics.

4. (10 minutes) During the last ten minutes of the class, have each student, on a clean sheet of notebook paper, draw his or her favorite bird and list its characteristics. Collect what they have done today, with the exception of their drawings, which will be due at the beginning of Wednesday's class.

Of great help in explaining an assignment to a class, particularly a multiple-part assignment, is for the substitute to list on the board the main parts of the assignment. That way you won't get a multitude of questions similar to "What do we do after the video?" and "How many birds did you say we had to write down and what are we supposed to write?"

When having a substitute give a test, adequate instructions should be left for the substitute:

Give the attached test on Chapter 20.

Students may not use their books or notes—have them take everything off their desks except their tests.

Test will take approximately twenty-five minutes, but some may take longer or less.

Have students write on the test.

Collect each test as the student completes it and then have the students who are finished read silently pages 125–135 (molecules) in their science books.

Inform students that any talking or cheating during or after the test will result in a zero (warn students first, and then leave me his or her name if the student commits a second offense).

As a substitute monitoring class behavior, you have to be aware of every student in the room. If the teacher has boxed the teacher's desk off in the corner of the room, hiding behind bookcases or some other barricade, you should stand or sit elsewhere so that you can observe every student in the room. Students scrunched down on the floor or in a corner of the room or sitting behind a barricade won't do. Students working behind a separate wall partition or students reading in the hall outside of the classroom can be a problem in monitoring class behavior. When you monitor kids you can't see, it becomes a matter of trust, rather than an objective observing. As a sub you usually don't know the kids well enough to know whom you can trust.

One hopes that, as a substitute, you won't be placed in a situation of "blind trust." Exceptions are many: yearbook, newspaper, photography, student government, drama, and a host of other classes that require classes to be broken up into smaller groups to go to various other places. It is up to the regular teacher to leave instructions on where and why kids should be out of sight. In such cases, often students have been placed in charge of activities or groups and it may turn out to be a pleasant situation. School newspaper editors, as an example, are usually wonderful in keeping kids on track while you are just there as the "adult presence."

In presenting a lesson to the "usual class" of thirty or so students in a "normal class," awareness of every student applies. The kid up-front who recites may not be heard by the student in the back of the room. While you get bogged down with a mini-discussion with two students on one side of the room, the rest of the class may drift off into talking and not paying attention. Awareness of all students and bringing them into the flow of the lesson is a way to minimize discipline problems and maximize learning.

"Gretchen is telling me up here that 37.5 is the correct answer. What do you ladies in the back think? Is she right?"

Your physical presence can help refocus a student or students who have drifted off into conversation while most members of the class are in focus with the lesson. Just move over by the two kids who are talking. Your physical presence usually gives them the message that they are being disruptive.

Moving about the room also causes students who are reciting to speak up so that you can hear them, providing you are not standing right next to the reciting student. "Chad, I'm sorry but I can't hear you. Could you turn a little more toward the class and speak up?"

Awareness! Awareness! Awareness of all of the class members! It is a skill that good teachers, regular and substitute, develop over time.

In some rooms, kids write all over desks. Other rooms have desks that are perfectly clean. What you do as a substitute is try to follow the pattern that has been set by the regular teacher. There is no sense in chastising a kid for drawing on a desk when every desk in the room is a monument to graffiti. If desks are clean and it is fairly obvious that students are not permitted to write on them, sometimes all it takes is walking over to a desk where a student is scribbling and tapping your finger on the desk while you go on with the lesson. At other times, it may take the admonishment "Get it off, please." Beyond that, you may have to leave the notation to the regular teacher: "Jerry Caldwell, period 2, wrote all over his desk and wouldn't stop when I asked him to."

Leaving good notes for the regular teacher is a responsibility of the substitute. Sometimes all it takes is the notation "Kids in all classes did a nice job. No problems. Thanks for a nice day."

Other times may take more reporting. "Periods 1, 2, 3, and 6 were great, but period 5 was difficult to handle and I didn't get through the entire lesson. We left off at page 27 instead of completing all of the assigned work. Here are several names of the troublemakers who disrupted the class: Steve Willows, Cheryl Bumgarten, Alex Madrid, Jessica Martin. These four people insisted on talking and not paying attention."

As a substitute, you are responsible for reporting back to the regular teacher enough information that the regular teacher knows what you did and can pick it up the next day without any problems:

Finished lesson 5 (collected papers).

Left video set where all classes left off except period 2. Had fire drill during period 2. Period 2 did finish lesson 5, but did not get to watch any of the video.

All classes were well behaved, but period 3 was a little difficult to settle down after the fire drill.

Sometimes regular teachers will not want to hear what you feel you must say in your report. They are professionals, and after all, "you are just a sub" in the eyes of the regular teacher. This line of reasoning does not alter the fact that sometimes the regular teacher knows less about teaching than the substitute knows.

Be diplomatic in your report. Instead of "Your students were rude, arrogant, totally out-of-control, lazy, and uncooperative," use something like "I had a difficult day. You must have your hands full with some of these kids. I don't envy you dealing with them on a day-to-day basis." The regular teacher gets the message and is more likely to respond to the criticism of the students than if you hit the regular teacher with both barrels, making the regular teacher feel like an incompetent.

Often, how a report is written is as important as what the report says. Show concern for the regular teacher's feelings. Use a little tact. The regular teacher probably knows that he or she has the biggest bunch of "turkeys" since public education began; you don't have to beat the regular teacher over the head with that fact in your report.

Your report is to inform the regular teacher what went on during his or her absence; it is not to pass judgment on the regular teacher. "You are one of the worst teachers for whom I have ever substituted. Your lesson plan was a joke, and you obviously have no classroom control. I'll never substitute for you again, so please don't request me." Inappropriate and not for the purpose for which a substitute report is intended. Inform the regular teacher what transpired on a particular day; don't make evaluations that set you up as an educational expert for things about which you may know very little.

In writing your report to the regular teacher, remember that the regular teacher operates under time constraints, as you do. After having a sub, a regular teacher does not want to come in and read a five-page report while getting ready for first hour. Be concise, convey necessary information, but don't run on with a college dissertation. Make it easy for the regular teacher to pick it up where you left off, just as, hopefully, the regular teacher made it easy for you to come in and pick it up where he or she left off.

The regular teacher also owes the sub the courtesy of reading the report and taking it seriously. Sub reports can be a valuable source of feedback that can help a regular teacher improve the learning environment. Maybe he or she won't need a sub again until three months later, but in the meantime, did the sub's report give the teacher any ideas for improvement? Furthermore, did the sub seem comfortable with the type of lesson plan and instructions that were left? Is there something the teacher could change for the next sub he or she has?

A long-term substitute assignment involves a change of tactics from a short-term assignment. The substitute must assume more of the role of the regular teacher. Perhaps the regular teacher is out for six weeks on maternity leave or is out four weeks recovering from surgery. For that length of time, the substitute must be "the teacher."

On a one- or two-day substitute assignment the substitute attempts to walk in the shoes of the regular teacher. As the period of time is extended, the shoes begin to pinch more and more. No two individuals can teach class exactly the same. Successful teaching is a blending of the individual teacher's personality with the "personality" of the class and the subject matter. What works for one teacher doesn't necessarily work for another. The longer the substitute tries to fit into the personality of the regular teacher, the more difficult it becomes to do so.

When taking over a class that has been in operation for quite some time, where the class expectations and educational pattern have been set, it is suggested that the long-term sub go slowly in changing that pattern. As the days extend, modify the pattern to suit your own needs and personality, remembering that at some point the class will be returned to the regular teacher, unless it is an end-of-the-year assignment.

In the case of a teacher who has been run out of the class by unruly students and who will not return, you may wish to establish your own standards quickly. Abrupt changes are likely to bring howls from the class and perhaps even the parents. You will need to do a balancing act, instituting the changes that are necessary to bring the class under control and establish a sound educational pattern, without having the class and the parents revolt so much that you fall victim to the same thing that happened to the regular teacher.

If the regular teacher is expected to return, you should fit your grading into the regular teacher's method. This will ensure an easy return to the classroom for the regular teacher in the area of grading, with minimal student and parent complaints about variations.

Lesson plans are a different matter. For an extended period of time, a substitute cannot be expected to exactly follow a regular teacher's lesson plans. The shoes get more uncomfortable and difficult for the substitute to walk in. A substitute has to be able to gradually shift lesson plans to what is comfortable and successful for him or her.

"Ms. Mallory will be out for eight weeks, but don't worry about making lesson plans. She will fax them to you at the beginning of each week. All you have to do is follow them."

Bad idea. Lesson plans are rarely a static commodity. They should be changed to fit whatever situation arises and to conform to the interaction of teacher and students. Lock-step curriculums, where all teachers are expected to be on the same page at the same time, are a formula for stagnation and decay.

"Here is the curriculum guide. You figure out how to teach it and make sure the kids learn it. You are a professional who knows how to get the job done." Direction, without requiring teachers to be robots, is the way to successful learning.

Long-term substitutes, like regular teachers, need the freedom to make the curriculum come alive. Teachers need guidelines of where they should go so that they don't wander off into no man's land, but how they accomplish the task of getting the curriculum across to students should be left to the individual teacher—that is what being a "professional" is all about.

A regular teacher will make many lesson plans during a teaching career. A substitute who substitutes for any length of time will follow many lesson plans made by many different teachers. All lesson plans are not created equal. A substitute can hope for the best, and, one hopes, "roll with the punches" when a lesson plan is not the best.

Chapter Three Summary of Suggestions

1. Regular teachers should remember that the lesson plans they make for a substitute are for another person, not for themselves.

2. Lesson plans made for a substitute should be clear, concise, and not bogged down in details.

3. Regular teachers need to remember that a good lesson plan for them might not be a good lesson plan for a substitute.

4. Plans made for a substitute should be easy to read.

5. Lesson plans made for a substitute should not be written on the board, unless a back-up copy on paper exists.

6. Lesson plans for a substitute should not be written on an overhead transparency and left on an overhead projector.

7. Sending a fax may not be a good way to get lesson plans to a substitute.

8. Giving lesson plans to a substitute by telephone is usually not advisable.

9. A substitute should be provided with a written set of lesson plans.

10. A backup lesson plan that does not depend on student participation should be provided when a substitute is left a lesson plan that depends on student participation.

11. Lesson plans left for a substitute that involve student participation should not be overly complicated and not overly involve the substitute.

12. A short-term substitute should never be required to grade a student.

13. A short-term substitute should never be required to give grades, complete a checklist on each student, or engage in any activity that takes the substitute's focus away from ensuring that the classroom is an orderly place of learning.

14. Regular teachers should not expect substitutes to carry out overly complicated games or "wild activities."

15. When a lesson plan calls for an overly complicated game or "wild activity," the substitute should modify the plan or shut down the activity as needed to keep kids under control.

16. Teachers' grade books and attendance books should not be left for a substitute.

17. Class lists and seating charts should be provided to a substitute.

18. Substitutes should leave for the regular teacher a list of absentees, as well as follow any school attendance procedures.

19. Lesson plans left for a substitute should not be overly complex.

20. Teachers leaving an audiovisual plan for a substitute should also leave a non-audiovisual backup lesson plan in case the audiovisual assignment can't be carried out.

21. Teachers leaving an audiovisual lesson plan for a substitute should:
    • Make sure the equipment is readily available and leave adequate instructions for its operation.
    • Prepare the class for the audiovisual assignment and leave adequate instructions for the substitute on the execution of the assignment.

22. A regular teacher should not regard a substitute audiovisual day as a "free period" day or visitation day for students.

23. Lesson plans left for a substitute should not contain a great deal more than students can accomplish, unless some of the work is expected to be completed as homework.

24. Lesson plans left for a substitute should not contain a great deal less than students can accomplish, leaving students with little to do during the class period.

25. If in doubt as to how long it will take students to complete work, the regular teacher should assign more work rather than less.

26. An end-of-the-period deadline to hand in work is usually a good idea.

27. A two-part lesson plan, requiring work to be handed in at the end of the period and other work to be started in class and completed at home is usually a good idea.

28. Long periods, particularly "block periods," may require several assignments or activities to keep students interested and focused.

29. When giving a multi-part assignment, it is a good idea to list the main parts of the assignment on the board to avoid student confusion.

30. The regular teacher, when having a substitute give a test, should leave adequate instructions on how to give the test.

31. To adequately monitor student behavior, position yourself where you can observe every student in the room.

32. When presenting a lesson, be aware of every student in the room and keep all students focused on the learning.

33. Moving close to disruptive students can sometimes get them to behave better and refocus on learning.

34. Moving yourself about the room, instead of remaining stationary in front of the class, can be helpful in getting students to speak loudly enough that the other students can hear them.

35. When you observe students writing on desks, follow the pattern that seems to have been set by the regular teacher. If other desks are clean, tell the student doodler to stop scribbling on it; if other desks have markings on them, ignore the desk writer.

36. Leave good notes for the regular teacher, informative but not excessively long.

37. Be diplomatic in your report to the regular teacher, providing necessary information without being savagely critical.

38. The regular teacher should read the sub's report and take it seriously, using it as a source for future improvement if possible.

39. A long-term assignment involves changing some of your tactics from what you normally do as a short-term substitute.

40. With a long-term substitute assignment, you need to gradually, rather than abruptly, change the teaching pattern to fit your needs and teaching style, instead of being tied to the needs and style of the teacher for whom you are substituting.

41. If the regular teacher is expected to return at some time after a long-term absence, fit your grading into the regular teacher's method of grading.

42. As a long-term substitute, make your own lesson plans, rather than having the absent teacher or someone else make them for you.

43. Although states and school districts set guidelines for what is to be taught, teachers, including long-term substitutes, should be free to make lesson plans that they feel are the most effective in educating students.

Chapter Four

Your Comfort Level

Your comfort level can be divided into two parts, your physical comfort and your emotional comfort. Your physical comfort involves those things in your environment that make you physically comfortable, external things that you either add to your environment or attempt to keep out of your environment. Your emotional comfort is within yourself, an attitude, a mental outlook that enables you to survive in the tough world of teaching without becoming a physical or emotional wreck.

Physical Comfort

Some things that raise the physical comfort level of a substitute are as basic as food and water. Carry your own water in your tote bag. This gives you access to water when you want it and helps you avoid school drinking fountains, which, on occasion, may be particularly nasty. Ever see a high school drinking fountain where someone has spit a wad of chewing tobacco? Ever see a middle school drinking fountain where someone has plugged it up with a wad of bubble gum? Many items are found in school fountains that make the fountains hazardous to your health.

Your tote bag, purse, briefcase, backpack, or whatever, might also include cough drops. A dry throat that leaves you gasping in front of a class can sometimes be quickly cured with a cough drop, and, if needed, a shot of water. Breath mints, gum, and other items are optional, although gum should not be chewed in front of students, since most schools have a prohibition against gum. Wandering around the classroom with a coffee cup or soft-drink can in your hand is also not recommended. In addition to students wanting to have the same, it damages the professional image you may be trying to create.

Food from school cafeterias may also be something you want to avoid, depending on how familiar you are with the school and how much hassle you are willing to put up with to get through the lunch line. In some schools, you may be able to get through the line quickly enough and into the faculty lunchroom so that it is worth the trouble it takes. In other schools, it may be more of a hassle than it's worth. It comes down to a matter of personal preference.

As a substitute, your lunch schedule can swing wildly from one day to the next. Your lunch schedule yesterday was 10:20–11:00; today, it's 12:40–1:10; different schools, different teachers—you may want to carry your lunch with you.

A breakfast bar or two and a piece of fruit are fast and convenient, although not gourmet. You may need to eat quickly and under varying circumstances. You may only have fifteen minutes to eat today because the assembly in the auditorium ran fifteen minutes longer than scheduled and you then had to come back to the room to let students in to get their backpacks. Eat in the classroom before your next class, popping in a breakfast bar and finishing up with an apple. It comes down to a matter of personal preference, necessity, and convenience.

Often very inconvenient is the necessity for your other biological needs. On some teachers' schedules, you may have more than adequate opportunity and time to take care of your bathroom needs. On other schedules, you may have little or no time for a bathroom break. As a teacher, you can't leave a class unattended any time the need arises. Some career teachers look forward to one of the benefits of retirement as being able to go to the bathroom whenever they want to.

As a substitute who frequently faces different schedules, planning ahead is important. When you get the teacher's schedule for the day, check two things: break times and bathroom locations.

Passing periods are not good for your bathroom breaks because they are short and you need to monitor students entering the room. Passing periods can be used for emergencies, but they are usually not the best.

Planning periods and lunch are the best opportunities to take care of personal needs. You can hope that the teacher's schedule will have them spaced for your convenience during the day. If not, you may have to resort to a passing period at some point.

Some schools have adequate faculty restrooms; some do not. Sometimes they are locked, and to gain admittance you must have a key, which, as a sub, you usually don't have. Faculty bathrooms don't seem to have been a high priority in the planning that went into some schools. Newer schools will usually have adequate faculty bathrooms, but in some older schools some bathrooms, faculty and student, have been converted into storage rooms, work rooms, or other uses. Adult faculty members should have separate bathrooms from students, but this is not always the case, so you may have to resort to the use of the student bathroom.

Student bathrooms, particularly at the high school level, can be the hell holes of Western Civilization. If a large number of facilities are provided, invariably, it seems that only one or two hand dryers are provided. With no paper towels and with an inadequate number of air dryers, many, if not most, students go on their way without washing their hands. Since the bathroom is often a disgrace from the standpoint of cleanliness, it raises a legitimate health concern.

As a substitute, you may wish to avoid handling frequently used student passes, preferring to have the students place them on a table or on some other convenient location, rather than handling them yourself and passing them on to another student. The same is true when collecting papers. Do you really want to handle all of those papers kids with runny noses are handing in? How about having the kids place their completed work on a chair at the front of the room? Some teachers already have folders or a particular place where kids hand in work. If so, use it.

Taking health precautions, since you are exposed to so many different students, can be as simple as moving a tissue box away from the teacher's desk to some other place in the room where students can conveniently use it. Kids are always blowing their noses, but they don't have to do it right next to you. When you leave, place the tissue box back on the teacher's desk, if that is where the regular teacher had it. If the regular teacher wants to be exposed to kids blowing their noses, that's the teacher's business. Besides, it helps keep the substitutes in jobs.

Whether it is a box of tissues on a teacher's desk that you move or something else, things should be returned to their usual places when you leave the room. The regular teacher should not have to look all over the room for markers, chalk, or erasers you have placed in the teacher's desk so that kids wouldn't write all over the board when they came into the room. Yes, kids today will do that sort of thing without asking your permission.

Is nothing sacred today, not even the teacher's chalkboard? No, very little, if anything. Some students are inclined to sit down at the teacher's desk, go through desk drawers, whatever, if you don't shoo them away, particularly with a substitute. Some high schools even have trouble keeping students out of faculty restrooms that are clearly marked "FACULTY." Of course, when student bathrooms have toilet paper plugging up the toilets, have mirrors missing because students have broken them, have no soap available because students can't handle the awesome responsibility of using soap properly, it is understandable why some students might prefer a faculty restroom.

As a substitute, your physical comfort varies from school to school and room to room. Rooms run from hot to cold, and usually you will have no way of adjusting the heat, which is often preset. Take a light jacket, sweater, or slip-on shirt to help you avoid the unexpected cold that may engulf you. Rooms that run hot present a harder problem to solve, but opening a window sometimes helps. Of course, when a school maintenance worker fires up a lawn mower to cut the grass right outside the room, you will probably have to close open windows so that the kids can hear you while they are sweating and you are shouting.

When deciding what to wear, take into consideration your physical comfort and what is appropriate. Take your cue from the faculty members of the schools where you substitute. Dress the part, and your comfort level should go up. Dressing similar to other faculty members will increase your chances of being accepted by students as a "regular teacher." If you show up looking like a derelict in a school where most teachers dress reasonably well, you will look and feel out of place. Although faculty dress standards no longer mandate suits and ties for males and dresses for females, as was the case thirty or forty years ago, many teachers dress nicely as well as comfortably. Let common sense and personal preference be your guide.

Emotional Comfort

Knowing where you are and where you should be at a particular time can contribute to your physical as well as emotional comfort. If it is a small school or a school you have substituted at a dozen times, where you are and where you should be at a particular time are usually of little concern. In the case of a large, unfamiliar school, jotting down the teacher's schedule and room number or room numbers may give you a sense of comfort when you travel elsewhere in the building. "When does the next class start and what room does she move to?" No problem. Pull the slip right out of your shirt pocket and look at it. "That's right. I go to hall duty on the southwest lower floor after lunch. I don't go back to room 211 until 1:10, after hall duty."

A few pencils and blank sheets of paper in your tote bag can, at times, provide some degree of physical and emotional comfort. The regular teacher didn't leave you a pencil to fill in the bubble attendance sheets. No problem; use your own. You need to leave for the regular teacher the names of students who left class at 1:30, claiming they were in the band concert. No paper for you to use in the classroom; use your own.

Loaning pencils or giving paper to students to use can be a bottomless pit. It is your decision, but don't be surprised if you don't get your favorite pen back when you loan it to a student. As a substitute, you probably won't be there the next day to remind the student, who has probably lost it by then anyway, to give it back. Alternate choice: "Ben says he doesn't have anything to write with. Anyone in class have a pencil he can borrow? No paper either, Ben? Well, see if someone will lend you a piece."

Being on time can contribute greatly to a teacher's comfort level. Traffic was terrible because the weather dropped buckets of snow on the streets overnight. You didn't allow extra time, so you are late or just barely in time to start the class. As a regular teacher, you are familiar enough with the routine that you make it through the class period, maybe not quite as well as when you have a few minutes to get set, but you still get the job done. As a substitute, you need every minute you can get to familiarize yourself before class. Today, you have no time to get set. Your discomfort level goes up, and your performance level goes down.

Sometimes, it is not the substitute's fault he or she is late. The call didn't come until late. The regular teacher labored under the burden of thinking he would be in school that day, but when his headache got so bad that he could hardly stand the pain, in spite of maximum-pain-relief tablets, he decided to call for a sub. Subs, although accustomed to responding quickly, are not superheroes. They require time to get ready and get from one place to another. Thus, as a courtesy, regular teachers should, whenever possible, put in a request for a sub as soon as an absence becomes definite.

This does not mean that a regular teacher should request a substitute a week or several days in advance on the premise that he or she might be absent. The substitute, given that assignment a week in advance, holds the assignment until the regular teacher cancels at the last day. The sub is then left without a job for that day, too late to get another assignment, having turned down other sub job offers that may have come in. No sub day + no job pay = unhappy sub who was cheated out of a workday and pay by an inconsiderate regular teacher.

Substitutes, when canceling previously assigned jobs, also owe the regular teacher courtesy. If the regular teacher has requested a particular sub and the sub has accepted, the regular teacher deserves to know when the sub can't make it. Regular teachers don't appreciate being "stood up" by a sub.

Many of the larger school systems have gone to an automated calling system, sometimes called "The Sub Finder." This makes things more convenient (or less), more impersonal, and easier to accept or refuse an assignment. A few pokes at the touch-tone phone and the substitute hears the details of the job and accepts or rejects the assignment. No friendly conversation with the school secretary, but the automation leaves the school secretary free to do other things, and the potential substitute is freed from making up phony excuses as to why he or she doesn't want to sub at a particular school or for a particular teacher.

The comfort level of the substitute can be greatly enhanced by calling the substitute finder, rather than waiting for the substitute finder to call you. Waiting for the sub finder to call you leaves you with job offers that haven't been "picked off" by other substitutes. Do your own "picking." Call the sub finder the day before you want to sub and see what it has to offer. Choose what you want, if anything is available; reject what you don't want. Sometimes, you can set up a number of different jobs on different days with a single call to the sub finder.

Calling the sub finder in advance helps avoid that miserable feeling of being roused from a sound sleep at 5:00, 6:00, or even later in the morning when you have convinced yourself that no sub jobs are available and you are going to sleep in. Under such conditions, the temptation is great to press the number that rejects the job. You start to drift back to sleep, and the sub finder calls again with a different job offer. Press the option that says you don't want any more calls that day and go back to sleep, if you can.

To avoid being called at all, take advantage of some of the other options in the sub finder menu. You want to take a few days off; plug it into the sub finder. You only want to work half days, in the morning; plug it into the sub finder. The sub finder has options that make it a wonderful friend, impersonal as it is. In school districts large enough to offer choices of substitute assignments, the substitute finder can raise your comfort level by giving you a large measure of control over your life as a substitute.

For regular teachers, the sub finder can also be a valuable friend. No hassle of explaining why you want to be off; just dial the sub finder and put in your request for a substitute on a particular day. The impersonal machine locates and schedules a sub, and you, the regular teacher, are worry-free.

As long as you correctly put in your request, if anything goes wrong, blame it on your impersonal friend. "I put in my request as prescribed. It wasn't my fault the stupid machine messed up. Why do we have a sub finder anyway? Why can't we just call Genevieve, the school secretary; she never broke down and messed things up." You have placed the blame on your impersonal friend, without ever hurting its feelings—after all, it is only a machine.

You, obviously, are not a machine. You have emotions, feelings; some might even think that teachers are human. If the truth were known, teachers may be the most human of all adults, for their world is the world of child and adolescent, where emotions are worn on sleeves and tantrum and tears are often only an instant away.

In this world of the young, teachers spend their days cut off from the adult world, with faculty-lounge chatter playing at being a part of the greater outside world. But your world can never be a part of the outside world, for you have chosen to be a part of the world of the young; and you have entombed yourself there, where children's attitudes, emotions, and thought patterns thrust at you daily, challenging your own sense of adulthood and keeping you insulated from the adult world.

You are a leader in the world of the child, but can you balance your heavy exposure to childhood with truly being an adult? Ever notice how some teachers take on many of the characteristics of the children they are expected to lead?

To keep your balance and maintain your sense of adulthood in the world of the young, be firm, fair, and friendly. You must be the guiding rudder that sets the example and does not succumb to petty emotions and juvenile antics. You are one of the most important role models for adulthood. Don't let them down by being as juvenile as they are.

As a leader of children, you will never do it perfectly. Mistakes are the human condition. Set yourself up for perfection and you are setting yourself up for disappointment. Spend too much time lamenting the mistakes you make, and it can eat away your sense of worth and your comfort level. When leading daily in the children's world, the regular teacher has an extremely difficult job. When substitutes pop into various children's societies, difficulty is compounded.

Be lenient with yourself. When you make a mistake and stumble, as you surely will, pick yourself up and go at it again. No matter how good a regular teacher or a substitute teacher you are, there will always be that occasional bad day. Learn from it, if possible, but don't brood over it. Put it in the past and go on with the future.

"To err is human. To forgive is divine." When it comes to teaching, don't expect divinity in yourself, but give yourself divinity by forgiving the errors of your ways.

Quick Checklist

Physical Comfort

1. Carry water.
2. Carry cough drops.
3. Carry breakfast bar or fruit.
4. Plan ahead for bathroom breaks.
5. Limit exposure to germs.
6. Carry a jacket or sweater.

Emotional Comfort

1. Use to your advantage the sub finder.
2. Be on time.
3. Jot down room numbers and times.
4. Carry a few pencils and blank sheets of paper.
5. Forgive yourself when you make mistakes.

Chapter Four Summary of Suggestions

1. Take your own water.
2. Have cough drops or some other item with you that can quell a dry throat or cough and keep you able to speak.
3. Don't chew gum in front of students or drink soft drinks or coffee while teaching class.
4. Carry a lunch or snack with you that can be quickly eaten if you have only a limited amount of time available to eat.
5. Look at your schedule for the day, observe where bathrooms are located, and plan when you will take a bathroom break or breaks.
6. Passing periods are not good for bathroom breaks.
7. Avoid handling frequently used student passes; instead, have students place them on a table or at some other convenient location.
8. You may wish to avoid handling papers that students are handing in.
9. Move away from the teacher's desk boxes of tissue that students take tissues from to blow their noses.
10. Before you leave the classroom, put things back where they were when you came into the room.
11. Carry a jacket, sweater, or slip-on shirt with you in case a classroom is cold and you can't adjust the heat.
12. When deciding what to wear, take into consideration your physical comfort and what is appropriate.
13. Observing what regular teachers wear can help a substitute decide what is appropriate to wear.

14. Dressing similar to what regular faculty members wear may help a substitute be accepted by students as a "regular teacher."

15. In a large, unfamiliar school, when temporarily leaving the classroom, jot down the room numbers and schedule of the teacher for whom you are substituting. Taking it with you may help you to not become confused about when you should return or be somewhere else.

16. When you substitute, have with you a few sheets of paper and pencils.

17. Asking whether anyone in a class will lend paper or a pencil to the student who has none may be a wise alternative to you "loaning" them.

18. Be on time.

19. Teachers who expect to be absent should request a substitute in adequate time for the substitute to be scheduled and get there.

20. Teachers should not request a substitute on the supposition that they *might* be absent and then cancel the request too late for the substitute to get another substitute assignment.

21. Substitutes, when canceling assignments where the regular teachers have specifically requested them, need to let the regular teacher know that they have canceled the assignment. The cancellation should be made soon enough that another substitute can be assigned to the job.

22. In school districts that have automated "sub finders," substitutes can benefit by calling the system and selecting jobs, rather than waiting for the "sub finder" to call them.

23. Both regular teachers and substitutes can benefit by taking advantage of the various options on the "sub finder" menu and using those options to fit their individual needs and situations.

24. In dealing with students, be firm, fair, and friendly.

25. Be an adult role model for students, rather than being as juvenile as your students.

26. Realize that you will make mistakes in the difficult job of teaching.

27. Be forgiving of yourself when you make mistakes.

28. Don't brood over mistakes; learn from them and put them in the past while you go on with the future.

29. Recognize that no matter how good a teacher you are, there will always be an occasional bad day.

30. When you have a bad day, pick yourself up, get on with the job of teaching, and enjoy the good days.

Chapter Five

The Importance of Substitute Teaching

The importance of substitute teaching in American public education is tremendous. "Tremendous" is a word that needs verification by statistics, but national statistics concerning substitute teaching are difficult to come by. It is much easier to find out how many computers we have for student use than it is to find out the number of substitute teachers and how many days they substitute each year in the nation's schools.

For those who require precise numbers and percentage-point calculations, it is hoped that you will be lenient with the following statistical analysis that attempts to verify by numbers the importance of substitute teaching. Perhaps if the importance of substitute teaching is ever fully recognized, the U.S. Department of Education and other agencies that collect data on public education will supply accurate statistics that reveal the depth of substitute teaching in the United States.

The school district of Jefferson County, Colorado, had an enrollment of 87,832 in the school year 2000–2001. The State of Colorado mandates a specific day each year to do an official count. Jefferson County is Colorado's largest school district in number of students.

The "JEFFCO Public Schools Substitute Teacher News" newsletter reported in its Spring 2001 edition that was sent to substitutes in June of that year:

> "During the 2000–2001 school year, we filled over 62,500 jobs through the automated system."

Jefferson County had approximately 5,300 teachers. This meant that the average number of times a substitute was called for each teacher was 11.79; in other words, approximately twelve times each year the students in any class had a substitute.

This is not a verifiable statistic because some of the substitute assignments were only for half a day. Other assignments were multiple days, even long-term. The gathering of accurate data on substitutes is a very tenuous undertaking for many reasons.

To accomplish the task of filling 62,500 substitute assignments, JEFFCO had somewhere between 1,000 to 2,000 substitutes available at different times, but with substitutes dropping in and out of the system, accurate numbers that reflect the norm are difficult to compute. The substitute newsletter reported: "Seventy-five substitutes each worked one hundred jobs or more during the 2000–2001 school year." Obviously, the vast majority of JEFFCO substitutes worked fewer than one hundred assignments during the year, but they also may have worked in other school districts, giving them a larger total of sub assignments.

Since there were 180 student-contact days during the nine-month school year, this means that, on average, 347 substitutes were needed each day in JEFFCO. On some days, five hundred subs may have been needed. Dividing 62,500 sub requests for the year by 180 gives an average of 347.22 substitutes needed each day.

Requests for substitutes fluctuate daily. Availability of substitutes fluctuates daily. Some subs sit idle, hoping for the sub call that never comes. Other days, there just aren't enough subs to go around; administrators and faculty scramble to cover classrooms where no sub could be found to take the place of the absent regular teacher.

Where did all of those teachers go? Sick days, personal days, professional meetings, teacher training, field trips, curriculum development, etc. Are teachers in Jefferson County, Colorado, any worse or any better than other districts across the nation in taking days off? Probably not. Some teachers rarely miss a day. Others use every sick-leave and personal day they get. Some teachers would far rather spend their time teaching class than being pulled out of class for required workshops or whatever. Other teachers are as meeting-happy as politicians and look for any excuse to abandon the classroom.

Is Jefferson County typical of other school districts in the United States? Who knows? JEFFCO is a suburban district that bumps up against the west side of the city of Denver and extends itself into the mountains. For the most part middle class to upper middle class, JEFFCO has pockets of poverty and pockets of wealth. Mostly Anglo, it has a large number of Hispanics, some Asian, and few Blacks. It consistently surpasses its neighbor, the Denver Public Schools, in test scores, but the Denver Public Schools are more inner-city and have more pockets of poverty than JEFFCO has. JEFFCO's test scores are more in line with those of the other suburban school districts that surround Denver.

To enter even shakier ground, let us project JEFFCO statistics onto the national scene. *The World Almanac and Book of Facts 2001* gives the number of public school teachers as 2,826,146 (Fall, 1998). Using the JEFFCO average of 11.79 substitute assignments per regular teacher per year and multiplying that by the number of U.S. teachers gives us 33,320,261. Thirty-three million sub assignments made in the United States each school year should give us some idea of the "tremendous" importance of substitute teaching in America's schools.

Is this analysis accurate? No, but I hope it gives an indication of the vast number of substitute assignments made in America's schools.

Who said the analysis would be perfect? What's another million, ten million, or whatever substitute assignments among teaching friends? Break out the computers and get accurate statistics. Help! We need mathematicians, calculus, Euclid, and theories of probability, not just some guy messing around with the fallacies of logic.

Millions of substitute assignments made each year—thirty-three million or whatever is the case. Substitutes are in front of the classroom a great deal of the time. Can we afford to throw away that teaching time? No. We need competent substitute teachers and competent regular teachers who know how to use substitutes properly.

Do school districts and states ensure that good substitutes will be in front of the class? Again, looking at Colorado as one example: "JEFFCO Public Schools Substitute Teacher News" newsletter, Spring 2001:

"The requirements for the One-Year Substitute Authorization from the state are at least a high school diploma and proof of successful experience working with children, including the signature of someone who verifies this experience and recommends the person for a license. The district requires that the person applying be at least 22 years of age."

Some good substitutes may come out of a licensing program such as this, but will most be qualified? Do we say, "Sure, you can fill in for a prosecuting attorney if you have a high school diploma and worked in a law office or court for a year and someone signs for you"? Do we hand you the surgical knife and let you operate because you have a high school diploma, worked at a hospital for a year, and your mother signs, saying that you are good at carving a pork roast?

It seems rather curious that, while there are constant outcries that regular teachers must be better qualified, the standards for substitute teachers remain, in many districts, minimal, and are often falling. Could it be the low pay and classroom abuse make it difficult to obtain and retain substitutes?

Pay, respect, and other things that attract good regular teachers are the same things that attract good substitute teachers. No one wants to be kicked in the stomach every day for a dime. Raise the rate to a quarter and you will have more applicants. Take away the stomach kicks and you will get people to hang out in the job longer. Some may even like it well enough to stick around for a long time.

Substitute teaching is important enough that it necessitates qualified people who are paid well and treated well. As a part of the goal of a quality education for every student, every absent teacher deserves a quality substitute.

Further complicating the analysis earlier in this chapter, the Substitute Teacher Office, in a very commendable effort to assist substitutes, produced a *Jefferson County Super Substitutes Back to School* booklet in the fall of 2001. The introductory letter by Jane Hammond, superintendent of the school district at that time, stated: "JEFFCO substitute teachers serve over 87,000 students in more than 135 schools. On average, approximately 450 substitutes are working in JEFFCO classrooms each day."

I bow to her statistic of 450, rather than 347, since she had far more information at her disposal than I did. This would indicate that the analysis earlier in the chapter underestimates the number of substitutes on any given day in JEFFCO and in the United States as a whole. It adds further weight to the primary point of this chapter—that substitutes are extremely important in American public education.

Chapter Five Summary of Suggestions

1. States and school districts should make a greater effort to ensure that any person who is given a substitute assignment is qualified to do the job.

2. To find qualified people to substitute, states and school districts should ensure that substitute pay is high enough to attract qualified people.

3. States, school districts, and the U.S. Department of Education should become more aware of the importance of substitute teaching, thereby raising the quality of substitute teaching and the achievement level of students.

Chapter Six

Is Substituting for You?

The most logical source of substitutes is former teachers, those who have done the job before and should know how to do it. Some former teachers have retired from the profession; others have merely dropped out to pursue other ends.

Why would retired teachers want to substitute? If they really wanted to teach, why wouldn't they have continued to do so as a regular teacher, whose pay is much higher and who enjoys a much higher level of respect?

Some of the benefits of substituting as opposed to regular teaching: part-time; work when you want to work; take time off when you want time off; no faculty meetings; no pressure for student achievement; no faculty politics; no grades to compute; when you leave your kids at the end of the day, your workday is over; no grading papers or lesson plans to make; no administrators breathing down your neck; accept or reject particular assignments; being a part of a school district without really being a part of it—sound contradictory?

As a substitute, you have become, in a sense, an independent operative. No more of this same room, same kids every day. You float from place to place, leaving unruly kids behind; you have become a free agent, called on to do a specialized job that crops up at different places—unless you are in a district that is so small as to have only one school.

With all of these wonderful aspects of substituting, why would retired teachers not want to substitute? "I've been there, done that" is a common reason. "Don't need the money. I just want to enjoy life." "I wouldn't go back into a classroom for all the gold in Fort Knox. I did my time in hell."

For retired teachers who take a turn at substituting but soon give it up, one of the chief reasons for not liking it is the change of status from regular teacher to substitute teacher. You felt some degree of control as a regular teacher. You ran a disciplined ship with your directions and standards being enforced. As a substitute, you are like the hired hand, taking directions from others. No more respect from the students because you no longer control the grades, have discipline measures at your fingertips, and can contact the parents; you are now just the one-day substitute the kids feel they can flip off with impunity.

For retired teachers who can change the mind-set from "regular" to "substitute," substituting can be a good way to supplement retirement income and remain active in teaching. For those who can't accept the loss of control and lack of respect that comes with going from "regular" to "substitute," substituting is not a good endeavor.

Former teachers who did not retire but left the profession for various reasons may find substituting beneficial as a part-time job. A mother with kids in school may find a two- or three-day work week very appealing. Although substitute pay is, in many districts, not terrific, it usually surpasses the retail wage. Being able to choose days off, working the same hours as the kids are in school, and not having a boss "ride herd over you" while you operate a cash register and stay until store closing can be an ideal way of earning money while fulfilling your role as a parent.

Former teachers who are pursuing other endeavors that don't suffice financially can also benefit from substituting. So you are into making pottery or running a crafts shop, substituting can ease the financial burden that your desired way of earning has created. Being creative is nice, but it doesn't always pay the bills.

Former teachers who may wish to return to the profession as regular teachers can also benefit from substituting. Hanging around a district as a substitute may get you well-enough known that you are given that teaching contract. Teacher B had to resign suddenly to move to a different state to take care of her aged father when her aunt, who was taking care of the father, died. Your sterling qualities as a substitute have become apparent to the principal of the school. You interview for the job and you are hired as a regular teacher.

Future teachers could also be a source of substitutes. Unfortunately, this is rarely the case. Becoming a teacher usually consists of college classes, student teaching, picking up your degree, and being hired as a regular teacher. Some teacher training programs in college are now emphasizing more time spent in the classroom before being certified.

As a part of that certification process, why not require time spent as a substitute? Before being hired as a regular teacher, as a final phase to being certified after student teaching, why not require a semester of substitute teaching under the direction of the college and the school district where the substituting takes place? The student who is going into teaching could make money as a substitute and gain valuable teaching experience before being hired as a regular teacher. Teaching from lesson plans made by many different teachers and being in many different classrooms could prove valuable to the person who is just entering the teaching profession.

A further benefit of requiring substitute teaching before becoming a regular teacher is that it would give school districts an opportunity to observe potential teaching candidates and to offer contracts to the ones they deem worthy. It would also be a way for school districts to detect weakness in a potential candidate and not offer a contract, or offer a contract with specific notations for improved performance before it would be renewed. This would also be a way of overcoming a substitute shortage in districts where one exists.

For districts that require less than a college degree to substitute, substituting is a legitimate way for a person to earn money and perhaps do something the person finds rewarding and satisfying. Substituting is usually too uncertain to be a full-time job, but in some cases, it can provide enough substitute days to be nearly full-time, particularly when a person substitutes in more than one district. District A may not call you for a job on Monday, but district B does. Some substitutes in a metropolitan area may be registered to substitute in several school districts, thus ensuring that they work practically every school day. Sometimes in the down time of summer, you can find substitute assignments in summer school or year-round school.

Whoever substitutes should be able to take the slings and arrows of substituting. If you are a person who can tolerate very little disrespect or "lip" from children and adolescents, substituting is probably not for you.

If you are a person who likes routine and very little variation, substituting may not be for you. Different schools, different schedules, different students—no set place or job each day—that is substituting. As a substitute you have to be able to adapt to many different situations.

Children—you don't have to love each of them, but you should be able to like most of them. Can you tolerate their juvenile behavior? Do you find them creatures of wonder or do their attempts to be "cute" cause you to break out in a rash? What is your reaction to kids and what is their reaction to you? Liking the product you are working with is important in substituting.

Do you believe teaching is important and is it something you want to do well? "I'm just substituting to make a few bucks and I couldn't care less what happens to kids and society in general." You may not feel that substituting puts you on a mission from God, but you need to at least feel that the mission is important. You won't save the world in one day of substituting, but is your little drop of energy one that adds to creating a better world?

As Shakespeare did not say, "To substitute or not to substitute, that is the question." Some do; some don't. Will you or won't you? Examine your own personal situation and decide.

One of the nice things about substituting is that it is not a lifetime commitment. Substituting is a day-to-day commitment. Commit yourself as you see fit. If it doesn't work out, then drop out. If you like it, stick around and enjoy it.

For those who want to make the commitment to regular teaching, but can't be hired where they want to teach because of a tight job market or whatever, substituting may open the door. Don't throw away that college degree and that teaching certificate that you worked so hard to earn. Hang on to substituting for a while, getting yourself known and proving your worth. It happens many times that substitutes, because of availability, persistence, and desire to teach, are hired as regular teachers.

Chapter Six Summary of Suggestions

1. Retired teachers are a good source of substitutes because they know how to do the job.

2. If you are a retired teacher, you may like substituting because:

    *   It is part-time, rather than full-time.
    *   You can take time off when you want to, choosing when you want to work.
    *   You do not have to attend faculty meetings.
    *   You are not pressured to get students to achieve.
    *   You are not involved in faculty politics.
    *   You do not have to grade papers or compute grades.
    *   When you leave at the end of the day, your workday is over.
    *   You do not have to make lesson plans.
    *   Administrators are usually not closely scrutinizing you or your work.

- You are free to accept or reject particular teaching assignments.
- You do not have to put up with the same unruly kids day after day.
- Substituting is a way for you to remain active in teaching, without experiencing all of the demands and pressures placed on full-time teachers.

3. If you are a retired teacher who decides to substitute, you will have to change your attitude from "regular teacher" to "substitute teacher."

4. Retired teachers who become substitute teachers have to be able to accept the fact that as substitutes they will receive less respect from students and have less control over students than when they were full-time teachers.

5. Former teachers who did not retire but left the profession for various reasons are a good source of substitutes because they have had experience on the job.

6. If you are a former teacher, you may like substituting because:
   - It is a way to supplement your income while pursuing other endeavors.
   - Its hours of work may be particularly suitable to your schedule, such as being a parent of school-age children.
   - Substitute pay usually surpasses pay in other part-time jobs, such as retail.
   - You may have a greater sense of freedom in substituting than in other part-time jobs.

7. If you wish to obtain a full-time teaching job, substituting is a good way to become well-enough known in a school district or at a particular school that you may be offered a position when one opens up.

8. After completing student teaching, prospective teachers could benefit from being required to substitute for a semester before being certified.

9. If substitute teaching becomes required of teacher-certification candidates, it should be under the supervision of the college they are attending and the school district that hires them as substitutes.

10. If teacher-certification candidates are required to substitute, they should be paid the same rate of pay as other substitutes in the school district.

11. You should not expect substitute teaching to be a full-time job.

12. If you wish to use substituting as a full-time way of earning, being registered to substitute in more than one school district at the same time will increase your opportunities for work and perhaps give you enough substitute assignments to make it full-time.

13. If you decide to substitute, you have to be able to tolerate some disrespect from children and adolescents.

14. If you prefer a job that gives you a sense of security by following the same routine every day, substituting is probably not a good choice for you.

15. As a substitute, you have to be able to adapt to different situations.

16. If you don't like children, you should probably not become a substitute.

17. If you don't think teaching is important, you should probably not become a substitute.

18. If you think substituting might be for you, try it.

19. If substituting doesn't work out for you, drop it; if substituting works for you, stay with it and enjoy it.

Chapter Seven

Emergency Lesson Plans

In constructing the lesson plans presented in the next four chapters, I set for myself the following criteria:

1. Must be short and direct, so simple that anyone of reasonable intelligence can quickly look at the plan and follow it with no difficulty.

2. Must require nothing other than each student having a pencil and paper.

3. Must make it easy for the fill-in teacher to maintain order.

4. Must engage the students for the entire period.

5. Must be general enough that it will fit the perceived subject matter.

6. Each lesson plan must stand on its own, without requiring a previous lesson plan or a continuing lesson plan.

7. Must be educational. Should not just consume time, but must produce educational benefit to students.

In looking at these lesson plans as a whole, they may, at times, seem repetitive in format. Don't worry about it. You are only teaching one lesson plan at a time, perhaps as many as three on three consecutive days. These are just fill-in, emergency plans, not the entire course in any case.

I have not set out to dazzle you with my brilliance (or lack thereof) at lesson planning. These are the nuts and bolts that will get you through an emergency situation. This is meat and potatoes stuff. If you want caviar or more spice in the classroom, there are many excellent books on the market that give you puzzles, games, and activities to occupy the students and your time. I am providing you with full-fledged lesson plans that focus on subject matter and keep the wheels of education rolling on a chartered course.

It is highly unlikely that students will stand up and cheer you at the end of a class period when you have used one of these plans. The outcome should be that you and they had a reasonable day of learning where you were in control and they learned something worthwhile related to the subject matter, without either you or the students enduring much stress.

Making lesson plans for the four core areas of grades 6 through 12 is a daunting, but not impossible task. Sticking to basics in each discipline, without the flair and fanfare of lesson plans that might be designed if teaching the class for an extended period of time, the task becomes workable by finding a framework for the lesson plans of each discipline.

Instead of a scattergun approach that pops you and the class into all kinds of activities, racing from breathless activity to breathless activity—yep, it's just basic stuff. Each lesson plan is a lifeline thrown out in an emergency situation. All you have to do is grasp it and let it pull you and the students safely through the class period.

In setting up the emergency lesson plans, I have attempted to follow commonly used curriculum in many school districts. School districts and individual schools vary in what is taught at what grade level. If, for example, I have emergency lesson plans for Grade 8, American History, and you happen to be called on to cover a Grade 9 class that is studying American History, by all means, use a Grade 8, American History plan with the ninth graders.

These plans were constructed to fill the "normal" secondary school period of about fifty minutes. They can be shortened or expanded in situations where classes are longer or shorter. Ever notice how TV weatherpersons do it when given less time or more time after the main part of the newscast? They verbally tap dance or verbally race, depending on the situation. Teachers do this sort of thing often.

So that you don't have to do much tap dancing, I have included an assignment that is due at the beginning of the next day's class period. Each student hands in his or her work when completed and then goes on to the assignment that is due at the beginning of the next class period.

Use these lesson plans when, and if, the need arises. I hope they will make your day easier at a particular place and time. Perhaps as a substitute teacher, or a middle school team member, or a high school department chairperson, or a school administrator, or a counselor, there will be a sense of security and confidence in keeping this book tucked away in an accessible place.

If the call comes, "Help! No lesson plans!" pull this book from its hidden place. Then with complete confidence, go forth and teach the masses!

Chapter Eight

English Lesson Plans

Grade 6, English
Understanding Literature, Lesson Plan 1

Preparing to work (about 5 minutes)

- Take roll if required to do so.
- Have each student take out a sheet of paper and place the usual classroom heading on it—name, and so on.
- Have students write the topic for the day at the top of their papers: *The Call of the Wild.*

Understanding the novel (about 20 minutes)

- Have the students *write* the following information on their papers while you make comments (if any) you wish to make:
    - A. Jack London's novel *The Call of the Wild* was published in 1903.
    - B. The setting of the book is the Alaska gold rush that took place when gold was discovered in 1897.
    - C. The story is told from the point of view of Buck, the powerful dog that experiences hardships, cruelty, love, and many other emotions.
    - D. Buck is ultimately faced with the decision of whether to remain with humans or join a wolf pack in the Alaskan wilderness.
- Read to the class the following brief summary of the novel:

    "Buck, a four-year-old, part St. Bernard and part Scotch Shepherd, weighing 140 pounds, is stolen from his California owner and shipped to Alaska. He becomes a sled dog, fighting for his place in the pack and enduring sometimes cruel treatment from his owners. He finally ends up living with a kind and loving owner, John Thornton. Living with Thornton and his gold-panning partners, Buck is torn between his desire to go into the wilderness and live as part of a wolf pack or stay with his human owner, John Thornton. Tragic events help Buck make his decision."

- Say to the class: "On your paper *write* three important things you think the author might be trying to tell readers."

Class discussion (about 10 minutes)

- Ask the class: "What are some of the things you think the author might be trying to communicate?"

Completing today's assignment (about 10 minutes)

- Have each student write a short paragraph on the same piece of paper he or she has been using. Start with the topic sentence: "One important thing that the novel communicates is that a dog responds to love."

After each student finishes today's work, it is to be handed in to you, and the student is to start the work that is due at the beginning of the period tomorrow.

- Tell students: "List five reasons why you might or might not like to read this book. Then write a paragraph on what you would expect to get from this book if you read it."

Grade 6, English
Understanding Literature, Lesson Plan 2

Preparing to work (about 5 minutes)

- Take roll if required to do so.
- Have each student take out a sheet of paper and place the usual classroom heading on it—name, and so on.
- Have students write the topic for the day at the top of their papers: *The Adventures of Tom Sawyer.*

Understanding the novel (about 20 minutes)

- Have students *write* the following information on their papers while you make comments (if any) you wish to make:
    A. Mark Twain's novel *The Adventures of Tom Sawyer* was published in 1876.
    B. The setting of the book is a small town on the Mississippi River where children of that era (mid-1800s) played and had adventures.

C. Tom Sawyer, being an adventurous boy, gets into mischief, predicaments, and situations that cause great concern to himself and others.

D. Tom, like all children of all times, has to deal with the restraints placed on him by adults while trying to live his life the way he wants to live it.

- Read to the class the following brief summary of the novel:

"Tom, while living with his Aunt Polly, truants school, gets into fights, teases girls, and plays in the woods with his freedom-loving and less-than-respectable friend Huck Finn. Tom tries to win the love of the new girl in school, Becky Thatcher. Tom and Huck witness a late-night murder in a graveyard. They run away with their friend Joe Harper. The three boys turn up at the funeral the town is holding, thinking that the runaways drowned in the river. Tom and Huck continue to worry about what will happen to them if anyone finds out what they saw in the graveyard. Tom and Becky get lost in a huge cave that has winding passages. The murderer is also in the cave. Tom and Huck eventually end up heroes."

- Say to the class: "On your paper *write* three important things you think the author might be trying to tell readers."

Class discussion (about 10 minutes)

- Ask the class: "What are some of the things you think the author might be trying to communicate?"

Completing today's assignment (about 10 minutes)

- Have each student write a short paragraph on the same piece of paper he or she has been using. Start with the topic sentence: "Tom Sawyer, even though living in the 1800s when life was different, has many things in common with children today."

After each student finishes today's work, it is to be handed in to you, and the student is to start the work that is due at the beginning of the period tomorrow.

- Tell students: "List five reasons why you might or might not like to read this book. Then write a paragraph on what you would expect from this book if you read it."

Grade 6, English
Understanding Literature, Lesson Plan 3

Preparing to work (about 5 minutes)

- Take roll if required to do so.

- Have each student take out a sheet of paper and place the usual classroom heading on it—name, and so on.
- Have the students *write* the topic of the day at the top of their papers: *A Connecticut Yankee in King Arthur's Court.*

Understanding the novel (about 20 minutes)

- Have students *write* the following information at the top of their papers while you make comments (if any) you wish to make:

    A. Mark Twain's novel *A Connecticut Yankee in King Arthur's Court* was published in 1889.

    B. Mark Twain was fascinated by the inventions and gadgets of his time.

    C. Mark Twain decided that sending a "modern man" back into time would make a good story.

    D. In the story, the "modern man" will use the inventions and his advanced knowledge for the good of the people.

- Read to the class the following brief summary of the novel:

    "Hank Morgan gets into a fight and is knocked out. When he wakes up, he is in the year 528. A knight in armor captures Hank and takes him to Camelot, where King Arthur and Queen Guinevere rule. On his way to be burned at the stake, Hank uses his modern knowledge of a solar eclipse to convince the King that he has remarkable powers. King Arthur makes Hank his chief magician. Hank becomes known as 'The Boss' and competes with Merlin in magic powers. Hank fights knights, falls in love, becomes a hero to the common people, and has many adventures before being returned to his own time."

- Say to the class: "On your paper *write* three important things you think the author might be trying to tell readers."

Class discussion (about 10 minutes)

- Ask the class: "What are some of the things you think the author might be trying to communicate?"

Completing today's assignment (about 10 minutes)

- Have each student write a short paragraph on the same piece of paper he or she has been using. Start with the topic sentence: "For Mark Twain, 1889 was modern, but 1889 wouldn't be modern today."

After each student finishes today's work, it is to be handed in to you, and the student is to start the work that is due at the beginning of the period tomorrow.

- Tell students: "List five reasons why you might or might not like to read this book. Then write a paragraph on what you would expect to get from this book if you read it."

Grade 7, English
Understanding Literature, Lesson Plan 1

Preparing to work (about 5 minutes)

- Take roll if required to do so.
- Have each student take out a sheet of paper and place the usual classroom heading on it—name, and so on.
- Have the students write the topic for the day at the top of their papers: *The Red Badge of Courage.*

Understanding the novel (about 20 minutes)

- Have students *write* the following information on their papers while you make comments (if any) you wish to make:
    - A. Stephen Crane's novel *The Red Badge of Courage* was published in 1895.
    - B. The story is about young Henry Fleming's experiences while fighting on the side of the Union during the Civil War.
    - C. Henry experiences fear and panic, but ultimately finds courage.
    - D. For Henry, there is a thin line between being a coward or being a hero.
- Read to the class the following brief summary of the novel:

    "Henry, serving with an infantry unit, wonders whether he will have the courage to face the enemy in battle or will he run away. In the first phase of the battle, Henry does not run, but when the battle is renewed, Henry flees in panic. Joining a column of wounded soldiers, Henry feels guilty and, while wrestling with his conscience, is struck on the head by the rifle of a man running from battle. Henry goes back to his regiment, where he lets them think that the blow to his head is a battle wound. His friends rejoice at seeing him alive. Henry finds the courage to become a ferocious warrior and leads the charge into battle."

- Say to the class: "On your paper *write* three important things you think the author might be trying to tell readers."

Class discussion (about 10 minutes)

- Ask the class: "What are some of the things you think the author might be trying to communicate?"

Completing today's assignment (about 10 minutes)

- Have each student write a short paragraph on the same piece of paper he or she has been using. Start with the topic sentence: "Henry Fleming was both a coward and a hero."

After each student finishes today's work, it is to be handed in to you, and the student is to start the work that is due at the beginning of the period tomorrow.

- Tell students: "List five reasons why you might or might not like to read this book. Then write a paragraph on what you would expect from this book if you read it."

Grade 7, English
Understanding Literature, Lesson Plan 2

Preparing to work (about 5 minutes)

- Take roll if required to do so.
- Have each student take out a sheet of paper and place the usual classroom heading on it—name, and so on.
- Have the students write the topic for the day at the top of their papers: *Uncle Tom's Cabin.*

Understanding the novel (about 20 minutes)

- Have students *write* the following information on their papers while you make comments (if any) you wish to make:
    A. Harriet Beecher Stowe's novel *Uncle Tom's Cabin* was published in 1852.
    B. The book was an overwhelming success and sold 300,000 copies the first year.
    C. The book depicted the evils of slavery and convinced many people that slavery should be abolished.
    D. Uncle Tom was a slave who lived his Christian faith by refusing to react in anger to those who abused him.
- Read to the class the following brief summary of the novel:

    "Mr. Shelby, who treats his slaves well, has financial difficulties and must give Uncle Tom and five-year-old Harry to a slave trader named Haley. Harry's mother, Eliza, flees with Harry to avoid being separated from her son. Uncle Tom refuses to go with them because he does not want to betray Mr. Shelby. Uncle Tom is eventually bought at a slave auction by Simon Legree, a cruel slave owner who taunts Uncle Tom about his religion, has Uncle Tom severely whipped, and does whatever he can to break Uncle Tom and his religious convictions. Uncle Tom does not forsake his religious convictions and give in to the will of Simon Legree. Uncle Tom is dying when Mr. Shelby's son George shows up to buy Uncle Tom back. Uncle Tom gives a prayer of thanks that he has not been forgotten by the Shelby family and dies."

- Say to the class: "On your paper *write* three important things you think the author might be trying to tell readers."

Class discussion (about 10 minutes)

- Ask the class: "What are some of the things you think the author might be trying to communicate?"

Completing today's assignment (about 10 minutes)

- Have each student write a short paragraph on the same piece of paper he or she has been using. Start with the topic sentence: "Uncle Tom was a powerfully built man, but he did not use his physical strength to fight."

After each student finishes today's work, it is to be handed in to you, and the student is to start the work that is due at the beginning of the period tomorrow.

- Tell students: "List five reasons why you might or might not like to read this book. Then write a paragraph on what you would expect from this book if you read it."

Grade 7, English
Understanding Literature, Lesson Plan 3

Preparing to work (about 5 minutes)

- Take roll if required to do so.
- Have each student take out a sheet of paper and place the usual classroom heading on it—name, and so on.
- Have the students write the topic for the day at the top of their papers: *Gone with the Wind.*

Understanding the novel (about 20 minutes)

- Have students *write* the following information on their papers while you make comments (if any) you wish to make:
    A. Margaret Mitchell's novel *Gone with the Wind* was published in 1936.
    B. The setting for the book is the area in and around Atlanta, before, during, and after the Civil War.
    C. The major character in the book is Scarlett O'Hara, who struggles with her emotions of love and the events that overtake the South.
    D. The South is destroyed by the war and Scarlett puts all of her strength into overcoming the misfortunes that have befallen her.

- Read to the class the following brief summary of the novel:

  "Sixteen-year-old Scarlett, daughter of a large plantation owner, is romantically pursued by many young men, but not Ashley Wilkes, whom she thinks she loves. Ashley marries Melanie. Scarlett, out of spite, marries Melanie's brother, Charles, who is soon killed in the war. Rhett Butler protects Scarlett, her little boy, Melanie and her baby, and the slave Prissy as the Yankees burn Atlanta. When the war ends, Scarlett vows to survive and rebuild the plantation. Through hardships, Scarlett manages to prosper, marrying men she doesn't love, only using them to climb back up in the world. Scarlett still thinks she is in love with Ashley, but finally realizes it is Rhett she really loves. Rhett, who has loved Scarlett all along, no longer cares and tells Scarlett he is going away for good. Scarlett vows to get him back."

- Say to the class: "On your paper *write* three important things you think the author might be trying to tell readers."

Class discussion (about 10 minutes)

- Ask the class: "What are some of the things you think the author might be trying to communicate?"

Completing today's assignment (about 10 minutes)

- Have each student write a short paragraph on the same piece of paper he or she has been using. Start with the topic sentence: "The Civil War changed the South forever."

After each student finishes today's work, it is to be handed in to you, and the student is to start the work that is due at the beginning of the period tomorrow.

- Tell students: "List five reasons why you might or might not like to read this book. Then write a paragraph on what you would expect from this book if you read it."

Grade 8, English
Understanding Literature, Lesson Plan 1

Preparing to work (about 5 minutes)

- Take roll if required to do so.
- Have each student take out a sheet of paper and place the usual classroom heading on it—name, and so on.

- Have the students write the topic for the day at the top of their papers: *The Adventures of Huckleberry Finn.*

Understanding the novel (about 20 minutes)

- Have students *write* the following information on their papers while you make comments (if any) you wish to make:

  A. Mark Twain's novel *The Adventures of Huckleberry Finn* was published in 1884.

  B. The story is about Huck, a boy who hates school and being restrained by conventional behavior, and Jim, a runaway slave.

  C. Jim and Huck float down the Mississippi on a raft.

  D. The river represents freedom for Jim, who is escaping from slavery, and freedom for Huck, who is escaping from society.

- Read to the class the following brief summary of the novel:

  > "Huck's father, Pap, is frequently drunk and, after beating Huck, locks him in a cabin. Huck breaks out of the cabin and fakes his death by killing a pig, spreading its blood in the cabin and leaving a bloody trail to the river. Pap and the townspeople think a robber killed Huck and threw his body into the river. Huck, while hiding out on an island, discovers Jim, a runaway slave, who is also hiding out on the island. The two of them become friends and decide to use a raft to float down the river. Along the way they have many adventures while trying to maintain their freedom."

- Say to the class: "On your paper *write* three important things you think the author might be trying to tell readers."

Class discussion (about 10 minutes)

- Ask the class: "What are some of the things you think the author might be trying to communicate?"

Completing today's assignment (about 10 minutes)

- Have each student write a short paragraph on the same piece of paper he or she has been using. Start with the topic sentence: "Although writing after the Civil War and the end of slavery, Mark Twain chose to set the novel before the Civil War to tell about freedom."

After each student finishes today's work, it is to be handed in to you, and the student is to start the work that is due at the beginning of the period tomorrow.

- Tell students: "List five reasons why you might or might not like to read this book. Then write a paragraph on what you would expect from this book if you read it."

Grade 8, English
Understanding Literature, Lesson Plan 2

Preparing to work (about 5 minutes)

- Take roll if required to do so.
- Have each student take out a sheet of paper and place the usual classroom heading on it—name, and so on.
- Have the students write the topic for the day at the top of their papers: *My Antonia.*

Understanding the novel (about 20 minutes)

- Have students *write* the following information on their papers while you make comments (if any) you wish to make:
    A. Willa Cather's novel *My Antonia* was published in 1918.
    B. The setting for the novel is the plains of Nebraska, where immigrant farmers settled, hoping to build a new life for themselves in America.
    C. The story is told by Jim Burden as he looks back years later and remembers the immigrant girl Antonia Shimerada.
    D. Jim is a New York lawyer, but he remembers growing up in Nebraska and the friendship, maybe even love, he shared with Antonia.
- Read to the class the following brief summary of the novel:

    "Orphaned at nine, ten-year-old Jim comes to Nebraska to live with his grandparents, who befriend the Shimerada family, recently arrived immigrants from Europe. Fourteen-year-old Antonia is the only member of the Shimerada family who is able to speak a little English. She and Jim become friends as they explore the prairie together, often on Jim's horse. Antonia's ability to speak English improves as Jim gives her English lessons. The harsh life of prairie farming and being homesick for his native land drives Mr. Shimerada to commit suicide. Antonia works in the fields, becomes a domestic servant, and does not go to school. Jim grows up, graduates from college, and moves away from Nebraska. Years later, he sees Antonia, remembering fondly their experiences, their love for the land, and Antonia's indomitable spirit and zest for living."

- Say to the class: "On your paper *write* three important things you think the author might be trying to tell readers."

Class discussion (about 10 minutes)

- Ask the class: "What are some of the things you think the author might be trying to communicate?"

Completing today's assignment (about 10 minutes)

- Have each student write a short paragraph on the same piece of paper he or she has been using. Start with the topic sentence: "Antonia was one of the immigrants who settled the plains and faced many challenges."

After each student finishes today's work, it is to be handed in to you, and the student is to start the work that is due at the beginning of the period tomorrow.

- Tell students: "List five reasons why you might or might not like to read this book. Then write a paragraph on what you would expect from this book if you read it."

Grade 8, English
Understanding Literature, Lesson Plan 3

Preparing to work (about 5 minutes)

- Take roll if required to do so.
- Have each student take out a sheet of paper and place the usual classroom heading on it—name, and so on.
- Have the students write the topic for the day at the top of their papers: *Death Comes for the Archbishop.*

Understanding the novel (about 20 minutes)

- Have students *write* the following information on their papers while you make comments (if any) you wish to make:
    A. Willa Cather's novel *Death Comes for the Archbishop* was published in 1927.
    B. The story begins two years after the United States has acquired the Southwest by defeating Mexico in war.
    C. Catholic Priest Jean Latour is appointed bishop of the New Mexico Territory.
    D. Bishop Latour is aided in his endeavors by his lifelong friend, Father Joseph Vaillant.
- Read to the class the following brief summary of the novel:

    "In 1850, the newly appointed Bishop Latour and his friend Father Valliant leave Ohio to take up their new duties in Santa Fe, New Mexico. After a very difficult journey that takes almost a year, they arrive in Santa Fe. They are not readily accepted by Mexican priests, who say they take orders from the Bishop of Durango in Mexico. Going to Durango, where his credentials have been sent, Bishop Latour returns to Santa Fe with the credentials and takes up his duties. Through years of struggle, ensuring justice and administering to the people of the Southwest, the Catholic Church grows and prospers. Shortly before his death, Archbishop Latour views the magnificent cathedral that has been built in Santa Fe and reflects on his life."

- Say to the class: "On your paper *write* three important things you think the author might be trying to tell readers."

Class discussion (about 10 minutes)

- Ask the class: "What are some of the things you think the author might be trying to communicate?"

Completing today's assignment (about 10 minutes)

- Have each student write a short paragraph on the same piece of paper he or she has been using. Start with the topic sentence: "Archbishop Latour was rich when he died, even though he did not own a lot of property or have a lot of money."

After each student finishes today's work, it is to be handed in to you, and the student is to start the work that is due at the beginning of the period tomorrow.

- Tell students: "List five reasons why you might or might not like to read this book. Then write a paragraph on what you would expect from this book if you read it."

Grade 9, English
Understanding Literature, Lesson Plan 1

Preparing to work (about 5 minutes)

- Take roll if required to do so.
- Have each student take out a sheet of paper and place the usual classroom heading on it—name, and so on.
- Have students write the topic for the day at the top of their papers: *The Grapes of Wrath*.

Understanding the novel (about 20 minutes)

- Have students *write* the following information on their papers while you make comments (if any) you wish to make:
    A. John Steinbeck's novel *The Grapes of Wrath* was published in 1939.
    B. The story takes place during the Great Depression of the 1930s when many people could not get jobs.

C. The story starts when Tom Joad is paroled from prison.

D. Drought and giant dust storms have ravaged Oklahoma and make it impossible for the Joad family to grow crops.

- Read to the class the following brief summary of the novel:

> "When Tom Joad reaches the family farm, he is told by a neighbor that the family has been evicted. Tom and a friend, Jim Casey, a former preacher, locate the family and they all pile in and on an old car that has been converted to a truck. They head west, hoping to reach California and jobs. The journey is arduous, with members of the family dying along the way. When they reach California, jobs are scarce and they are forced to take jobs at any pay and under any conditions. Being hated 'Okies,' they have difficulty with the police. Casey is clubbed to death, and Tom leaves the family, planning to continue Casey's attempt to form a labor union, even though he knows the police are looking for him."

- Say to the class: "On your paper *write* three important things you think the author might be trying to tell readers."

Class discussion (about 10 minutes)

- Ask the class: "What are some of the things you think the author might be trying to communicate?"

Completing today's assignment (about 10 minutes)

- Have each student write a short paragraph on the same piece of paper he or she has been using. Start with the topic sentence: "The 1930s were hard for many people."

After each student finishes today's work, it is to be handed in to you, and the student is to start the work that is due at the beginning of the period tomorrow.

- Tell students: "List five reasons why you might or might not like to read this book. Then write a paragraph on what you would expect from this book if you read it."

Grade 9, English
Understanding Literature, Lesson Plan 2

Preparing to work (about 5 minutes)

- Take roll if required to do so.
- Have each student take out a sheet of paper and place the usual classroom heading on it—name, and so on.
- Have students write the topic for the day at the top of their papers: *The Good Earth.*

Understanding the novel (about 20 minutes)

- Have students *write* the following information on their papers while you make comments (if any) you wish to make:
    - A. Pearl Buck's novel *The Good Earth* was published in 1931.
    - B. The story takes place in China in the early 1900s.
    - C. The story starts on Wang Lung's wedding day, when Wang, a poor farmer, marries, in an arranged marriage, O-Lan, a slave in the great house of Hwang.
    - D. Wang and O-Lan struggle through years of hardship.

- Read to the class the following brief summary of the novel:

    "Starting with his elderly father's small parcel of land, Wang Lung is able to acquire more land. The farm is successful for a while before a drought causes the crops to fail. Wang and his growing family go to a large city where they barely survive by begging for food. Wang gets a job pulling a ricksha, and through a surprising turn of events, they are able to buy the land owned by the great house of Hwang. They again prosper, but they have to overcome a great flood, a plague of grasshoppers, and a scheming uncle. Wang also creates tension within the family by bringing an attractive young woman to live with them when O-Lan has grown old and less physically attractive than when she was young."

- Say to the class: "On your paper *write* three important things you think the author might be trying to tell readers."

Class discussion (about 10 minutes)

- Ask the class: "What are some of the things you think the author might be trying to communicate?"

Completing today's assignment (about 10 minutes)

- Have each student write a short paragraph on the same piece of paper he or she has been using. Start with the topic sentence: "Life is often a struggle to survive, no matter where or when you live."

After each student finishes today's work, it is to be handed in to you, and the student is to start the work that is due at the beginning of the period tomorrow.

- Tell students: "List five reasons why you might or might not like to read this book. Then write a paragraph on what you would expect from this book if you read it."

Grade 9, English
Understanding Literature, Lesson Plan 3

Preparing to work (about 5 minutes)

- Take roll if required to do so.
- Have each student take out a sheet of paper and place the usual classroom heading on it—name, and so on.
- Have students write the topic for the day at the top of their papers: *Of Mice and Men.*

Understanding the novel (about 20 minutes)

- Have students *write* the following information on their papers while you make comments (if any) you wish to make:
    A. John Steinbeck's novel *Of Mice and Men* was published in 1937.
    B. The story takes place on a ranch in California.
    C. George and Lennie are hired to work at the ranch.
    D. George feels an obligation to take care of Lennie, who is mentally retarded.
- Read to the class the following brief summary of the novel:

    "When George and Lennie arrive at the ranch, George does the talking to try to hide Lennie's mental deficiency. In their spare time, Lennie always wants George to tell him how they are someday going to have their own place where Lennie can pet and take care of rabbits. Curley taunts Lennie and thinks he is an overgrown coward until George tells Lennie that it is O.K. to fight back. Lennie crushes Curley's hand. Lennie accidentally kills a puppy when he playfully slaps it as it nips at his fingers. Curley's wife likes to flirt with the men and Lennie accidentally kills her trying to stop her from screaming when he strokes her hair too hard. Lennie runs away and the ranch hands go looking for him. George finds Lennie before the others do, knowing what has to be done and wanting it done as humanely as possible."

- Say to the class: "On your paper *write* three important things you think the author might be trying to tell readers."

Class discussion (about 10 minutes)

- Ask the class: "What are some of the things you think the author might be trying to communicate?"

Completing today's assignment (about 10 minutes)

- Have each student write a short paragraph on the same piece of paper he or she has been using. Start with the topic sentence: "Sometimes well-intended actions can be misinterpreted."

After each student finishes today's work, it is to be handed in to you, and the student is to start the work that is due at the beginning of the period tomorrow.

- Tell students: "List five reasons why you might or might not like to read this book. Then write a paragraph on what you would expect from this book if you read it."

Grade 10, English
Understanding Literature, Lesson Plan 1

Preparing to work (about 5 minutes)

- Take roll if required to do so.
- Have each student take out a sheet of paper and place the usual classroom heading on it—name, and so on.
- Have students write the topic for the day at the top of their papers: *The Great Gatsby.*

Understanding the novel (about 20 minutes)

- Have students *write* the following information on their papers while you make comments (if any) you wish to make:
    - A. F. Scott Fitzgerald's novel *The Great Gatsby* was published in 1925.
    - B. The setting for the novel is a wealthy section of Long Island, New York, in 1922.
    - C. Nick Carraway, recently arrived in New York to take a job, rents a small house next to the estate of Jay Gatsby.
    - D. Gatsby is a mystery to the community, having great wealth, with those on adjoining estates knowing almost nothing about him.
- Read to the class the following brief summary of the novel:

    "Nick has dinner one evening with his cousin Daisy, her husband, Tom, and a young woman named Jordan. Daisy and Tom argue in another part of the house and Jordan tells Nick that their marriage is in trouble because Tom is having an affair. The mysterious Gatsby throws lavish parties and Nick is invited to one. Nick later finds out that Gatsby is seeking his friendship as a way to make contact with Daisy. Nick arranges a meeting between

Gatsby and Daisy. They were once young lovers and Gatsby, once poor, has bought a mansion, hosted parties, and done everything that money can buy to impress Daisy. As their renewed romance progresses, they run a dangerous course that leads to a fatal accident and murder."

- Say to the class: "On your paper *write* three important things you think the author might be trying to tell readers."

Class discussion (about 10 minutes)

- Ask the class: "What are some of the things you think the author might be trying to communicate?"

Completing today's assignment (about 10 minutes)

- Have each student write a short paragraph on the same piece of paper he or she has been using. Start with the topic sentence: "As time moves on, it is difficult to recapture the past."

After each student finishes today's work, it is to be handed in to you, and the student is to start the work that is due at the beginning of the period tomorrow.

- Tell students: "List five reasons why you might or might not like to read this book. Then write a paragraph on what you would expect from this book if you read it."

Grade 10, English
Understanding Literature, Lesson Plan 2

Preparing to work (about 5 minutes)

- Take roll if required to do so.
- Have each student take out a sheet of paper and place the usual classroom heading on it—name, and so on.
- Have students write the topic for the day at the top of their papers: *Native Son.*

Understanding the novel (about 20 minutes)

- Have students *write* the following information on their papers while you make comments (if any) you wish to make:
    A. Richard Wright's novel *Native Son* was published in 1940.
    B. The story takes place in Chicago.

    C. The main character is Bigger Thomas, a twenty-year-old black man who lives in the slums.

    D. Bigger has done time in reform school and has committed minor robberies with a gang.

- Read to the class the following brief summary of the novel:

> "Bigger applies for a job as a chauffeur for a wealthy white family and gets it. Bigger is supposed to drive the daughter Mary to the university, but she orders him to drive her to a place where they pick up her boyfriend, Jan. Jan drives the car and they go to a black neighborhood, insisting that Bigger accompany them when they go into a night spot to eat and drink. After Jan is dropped off, Bigger drives drunken Mary home and helps her to her room. When Mary's mother calls her, Bigger puts a pillow over Mary's face, hoping to quiet her as she lies on the bed. Bigger accidentally suffocates Mary. Bigger decides to burn the body in the furnace. Grotesque things happen until there is no way out for Bigger."

- Say to the class: "On your paper *write* three important things you think the author might be trying to tell readers."

Class discussion (about 10 minutes)

- Ask the class: "What are some of the things you think the author might be trying to communicate?"

Completing today's assignment (about 10 minutes)

- Have each student write a short paragraph on the same piece of paper he or she has been using. Start with the topic sentence: "Sometimes people mean well, but it doesn't always turn out well."

After each student finishes today's work, it is to be handed in to you, and the student is to start the work that is due at the beginning of the period tomorrow.

- Tell students: "List five reasons why you might or might not like to read this book. Then write a paragraph on what you would expect from this book if you read it."

Grade 10, English
Understanding Literature, Lesson Plan 3

Preparing to work (about 5 minutes)

- Take roll if required to do so.
- Have each student take out a sheet of paper and place the usual classroom heading on it—name, and so on.

- Have students write the topic for the day at the top of their papers: *The Catcher in the Rye.*

Understanding the novel (about 20 minutes)

- Have students *write* the following information on their papers while you make comments (if any) you wish to make:
  A. J. D. Salinger's novel *The Catcher in the Rye* was published in 1951.
  B. The main character is sixteen-year-old Holden Caulfield, who has been expelled from a number of schools.
  C. Holden is somewhat of a social misfit, caught between adolescence and the adult world.
  D. Holden goes through a number of experiences, none of which ever seems to turn out right.
- Read to the class the following brief summary of the novel:

  "Holden is expelled from yet another private school, where he is failing four of the five subjects he has been taking. Holden catches a train home to New York City. Holden is good at making up stories and tells the lady sitting next to him that he is returning home because he needs a brain operation. In New York City, he does not want to face his parents, so he checks into a hotel. Holden experiences a number of situations that turn out badly and finally goes home when his money runs out. His ten-year-old sister loans him the $8 she has saved to purchase Christmas gifts and Holden is again able to avoid his parents. He thinks of going west, getting a job as a gas station attendant, and pretending to be a deaf mute. Holden eventually ends up in psychiatric care."

- Say to the class: "On your paper *write* three important things you think the author might be trying to tell readers."

Class discussion (about 10 minutes)

- Ask the class: "What are some of the things you think the author might be trying to communicate?"

Completing today's assignment (about 10 minutes)

- Have each student write a short paragraph on the same piece of paper he or she has been using. Start with the topic sentence: "Going from adolescence to adulthood is sometimes very difficult."

After each student finishes today's work, it is to be handed in to you, and the student is to start the work that is due at the beginning of the period tomorrow.

- Tell students: "List five reasons why you might or might not like to read this book. Then write a paragraph on what you would expect from this book if you read it."

Grade 11, English
Understanding Literature, Lesson Plan 1

Preparing to work (about 5 minutes)

- Take roll if required to do so.
- Have each student take out a sheet of paper and place the usual classroom heading on it—name, and so on.
- Have students write the topic for the day at the top of their papers: *The Bridge of San Luis Rey.*

Understanding the novel (about 20 minutes)

- Have students *write* the following information on their papers while you make comments (if any) you wish to make:
  A. Thornton Wilder's novel *The Bridge of San Luis Rey* was published in 1927.
  B. The setting for the story is Peru in 1714 when a bridge between Lima and Cuzco collapses.
  C. Five people traveling across the bridge are killed.
  D. Brother Juniper, a Franciscan friar, sees the bridge fall.
- Read to the class the following brief summary of the novel:

  "Brother Juniper, a deeply religious man, believes that the five who died from the collapse of the bridge must have been chosen by God. To prove that God's hand is in our lives and in our deaths, he vows to learn everything he can about the five who died. It is his intention to gather the information into a book, proving that we live and die by design, rather than by accident. After six years, he has completed his task, with the life stories of each of the five. The three adults who died had an intense love for another person. Brother Juniper's book is declared heresy and he and the book are burned, but a secret copy remains at the university."

- Say to the class: "On your paper *write* three important things you think the author might be trying to tell readers."

Class discussion (about 10 minutes)

- Ask the class: "What are some of the things you think the author might be trying to communicate?"

Completing today's assignment (about 10 minutes)

- Have each student write a short paragraph on the same piece of paper he or she has been using. Start with the topic sentence: "Whether we live by design or accident is an interesting question."

After each student finishes today's work, it is to be handed in to you, and the student is to start the work that is due at the beginning of the period tomorrow.

- Tell students: "List five reasons why you might or might not like to read this book. Then write a paragraph on what you would expect from this book if you read it."

Grade 11, English
Understanding Literature, Lesson Plan 2

Preparing to work (about 5 minutes)

- Take roll if required to do so.
- Have each student take out a sheet of paper and place the usual classroom heading on it—name, and so on.
- Have students write the topic for the day at the top of their papers: *Moby-Dick.*

Understanding the novel (about 20 minutes)

- Have students *write* the following information on their papers while you make comments (if any) you wish to make:
    A. Herman Melville's novel *Moby-Dick* was published in 1851.
    B. The story involves a New England whaling ship and its Captain, Ahab.
    C. In the 1800s, sperm whales were hunted for their oil, the oil being used in lamps.
    D. Captain Ahab hates Moby-Dick, a white whale.
- Read to the class the following brief summary of the novel:

    "Ishmael, a merchant sailor, tells the story of shipping out on the *Pequod.* The whaling ship commanded by Captain Ahab sails from the seaport of Nantucket. The crew soon learns that Captain Ahab is more interested in finding Moby-Dick than he is in killing whales and bringing back a large amount of whale oil. A previous encounter with Moby-Dick is the reason for Ahab's wooden leg, and Ahab is obsessed with evening the score by killing Moby-Dick. After an extensive search, Moby-Dick is located. An intense battle between the whalers and Moby-Dick ensues. Moby-Dick proves that whaling harpoons and Captain Ahab are no match for his ability to survive, which seems supernatural."

- Say to the class: "On your paper *write* three important things you think the author might be trying to tell readers."

Class discussion (about 10 minutes)

- Ask the class: "What are some of the things you think the author might be trying to communicate?"

Completing today's assignment (about 10 minutes)

- Have each student write a short paragraph on the same piece of paper he or she has been using. Start with the topic sentence: "Revenge can be a dangerous obsession."

After each student finishes today's work, it is to be handed in to you, and the student is to start the work that is due at the beginning of the period tomorrow.

- Tell students: "List five reasons why you might or might not like to read this book. Then write a paragraph on what you would expect from this book if you read it."

Grade 11, English
Understanding Literature, Lesson Plan 3

Preparing to work (about 5 minutes)

- Take roll if required to do so.
- Have each student take out a sheet of paper and place the usual classroom heading on it—name, and so on.
- Have students write the topic for the day at the top of their papers: *The Scarlet Letter.*

Understanding the novel (about 20 minutes)

- Have students *write* the following information on their papers while you make comments (if any) you wish to make:
    A. Nathaniel Hawthorne's novel *The Scarlet Letter* was published in 1850.
    B. The setting is Colonial New England.
    C. The usual punishment for adultery was death.
    D. Hester Prynne receives a lenient sentence for adultery; she has to stand on a public platform for three hours and wear for the rest of her life a scarlet A.
- Read to the class the following brief summary of the novel:

> "When found guilty of adultery, Hester refuses to identify the father of her baby. The baby grows into a little girl with the Puritans thinking she may be an imp of the devil. Hester's husband, Roger Chillingworth, who had sent Hester ahead to the New World, arrives from England. Hester will not tell him who fathered Pearl. The Reverend Arthur Dimmesdale labors under his silent guilt of being the father of Pearl. Chillingworth eventually figures out that Dimmesdale is the father. Without revealing what he knows, Chillingworth mentally tortures Dimmesdale. Dimmesdale, finally no longer able to bear his guilt in silence, mounts the public platform with Hester and Pearl. He declares that he too bears the scarlet letter, which he has secretly worn on his chest under his outer clothing."

- Say to the class: "On your paper *write* three important things you think the author might be trying to tell readers."

Class discussion (about 10 minutes)

- Ask the class: "What are some of the things you think the author might be trying to communicate?"

Completing today's assignment (about 10 minutes)

- Have each student write a short paragraph on the same piece of paper he or she has been using. Start with the topic sentence: "Guilt can consume a person."

After each student finishes today's work, it is to be handed in to you, and the student is to start the work that is due at the beginning of the period tomorrow.

- Tell students: "List five reasons why you might or might not like to read this book. Then write a paragraph on what you would expect from this book if you read it."

Grade 12, English
Understanding Literature, Lesson Plan 1

Preparing to work (about 5 minutes)

- Take roll if required to do so.
- Have each student take out a sheet of paper and place the usual classroom heading on it—name, and so on.
- Have students write the topic for the day at the top of their papers: *For Whom the Bell Tolls.*

Understanding the novel (about 20 minutes)

- Have students *write* the following information on their papers while you make comments (if any) you wish to make:
    A. Ernest Hemingway's novel *For Whom the Bell Tolls* was published in 1940.
    B. The setting is the Spanish Civil War that took place shortly before World War II engulfed much of the world.
    C. Robert Jordan is an American who has voluntarily gone to Spain to fight.
    D. Jordan is willing to risk his life in a cause he thinks is just.
- Read to the class the following brief summary of the novel:

    "Jordan carries two heavy packs of explosives as he links up with a small band of guerrilla forces. Jordan's orders from those higher up in the chain of command are to blow up a bridge. The band of guerrillas is composed of members of various temperaments and commitment. Pilar, a middle-aged woman, is tough and committed to the cause. Pablo resents Jordan being there and is a problem for Jordan. Maria, a beautiful young woman, is immediately attracted to Jordan and romance develops. Overcoming various obstacles, the bridge is blown. Jordan's leg is broken as they flee. Jordan urges the others to go on without him, knowing that he will be killed by the enemy, but believing that he did the right thing."

- Say to the class: "On your paper *write* three important things you think the author might be trying to tell readers."

Class discussion (about 10 minutes)

- Ask the class: "What are some of the things you think the author might be trying to communicate?"

Completing today's assignment (about 10 minutes)

- Have each student write a short paragraph on the same piece of paper he or she has been using. Start with the topic sentence: "Dying for your beliefs is not an easy thing."

After each student finishes today's work, it is to be handed in to you, and the student is to start the work that is due at the beginning of the period tomorrow.

- Tell students: "List five reasons why you might or might not like to read this book. Then write a paragraph on what you would expect from this book if you read it."

Grade 12, English
Understanding Literature, Lesson Plan 2

Preparing to work (about 5 minutes)

- Take roll if required to do so.
- Have each student take out a sheet of paper and place the usual classroom heading on it—name, and so on.
- Have students write the topic for the day at the top of their papers: *Invisible Man.*

Understanding the novel (about 20 minutes)

- Have students *write* the following information on their papers while you make comments (if any) you wish to make:
  A. Ralph Ellison's novel *Invisible Man* was published in 1952.
  B. A nameless narrator tells the story, with himself being the main character.

C. The novel explores the status of blacks in society in relationship to whites.

D. The novel offers two main alternative responses by blacks to society: peaceful cooperation to achieve integration or violence and separation from whites.

- Read to the class the following brief summary of the novel:

> "The narrator attends a college for blacks in the South. Incurring the displeasure of the president of the college, the narrator goes to New York City and looks for work. After finding and losing a job with a company in the paint business, the narrator goes to work for the Brotherhood of Man, an organization dedicated to peaceful integration and equality. The Black Nationalist Party advocates violence and separation from whites. The narrator displeases both organizations. Caught in the middle of rival factions of blacks, the narrator witnesses riots and is in danger of being killed."

- Say to the class: "On your paper *write* three important things you think the author might be trying to tell readers."

Class discussion (about 10 minutes)

- Ask the class: "What are some of the things you think the author might be trying to communicate?"

Completing today's assignment (about 10 minutes)

- Have each student write a short paragraph on the same piece of paper he or she has been using. Start with the topic sentence: "*Invisible Man,* published in 1952, was a surprisingly accurate predictor of race relations in the 1960s."

After each student finishes today's work, it is to be handed in to you, and the student is to start the work that is due at the beginning of the period tomorrow.

- Tell students: "List five reasons why you might or might not like to read this book. Then write a paragraph on what you would expect to get from this book if you read it."

Grade 12, English
Understanding Literature, Lesson Plan 3

Preparing to work (about 5 minutes)

- Take roll if required to do so.
- Have each student take out a sheet of paper and place the usual classroom heading on it—name, and so on.
- Have students write the topic for the day at the top of their papers: *Light in August.*

Understanding the novel (about 20 minutes)

- Have students *write* the following information on their papers while you make comments (if any) you wish to make:

    A. William Faulkner's novel *Light in August* was published in 1932.

    B. The setting is rural Mississippi.

    C. Pregnant, twenty-year-old Lena Grove is searching for the father of her soon-to-be-born baby.

    D. The father was called "Lucas Burch" when he impregnated her.

- Read to the class the following brief summary of the novel:

    "Lena has walked and hitchhiked her way to the town of Jefferson, where she inquires for Lucas Burch at a mill that turns out lumber. Byron Bunch, a worker at the mill, has great sympathy for Lena; his sympathy quickly turns to love. Lucas Burch, now called "Joe Brown," is a bootlegger partner of Joe Christmas. Joe Christmas, part black and part white, in a rage over the white woman with whom he is having an affair suggesting he go to a Negro college, kills the woman. Brown burns down the woman's old mansion house, being too drunk to know whether or not he himself committed the murder. Brown flees the law, Lena, and her newborn baby. Lena and the baby continue to go in search of Brown. Byron Bunch continues to travel after Lena, watching out for her and the baby and loving her."

- Say to the class: "On your paper *write* three important things you think the author might be trying to tell readers."

Class discussion (about 10 minutes)

- Ask the class: "What are some of the things you think the author might be trying to communicate?"

Completing today's assignment (about 10 minutes)

- Have each student write a short paragraph on the same piece of paper he or she has been using. Start with the topic sentence: "Some people persist in pursuing a relationship that seems impossible."

After each student finishes today's work, it is to be handed in to you, and the student is to start the work that is due at the beginning of the period tomorrow.

- Tell students: "List five reasons why you might or might not like to read this book. Then write a paragraph on what you would expect from this book if you read it."

Chapter Nine

Math Lesson Plans

Note to Substitute: Math is a subject that has students of many different levels of ability working on many different types of problems. The closest match for a lesson plan that fits where students are working is to continue what the students have been doing, usually from a textbook. Thus, Lesson Plan 1 is a plan for doing just that. In case there is no text available or you prefer to do something other than have students solve problems from a book, three other lesson plans are included in which students construct their own problems: Lesson Plan 2 (individual problem solving), Lesson Plan 3 (partner problem solving), and Lesson Plan 4 (group problem solving). Any of the lesson plans should work with any grade level and any subject.

All Grade Levels, Math
Lesson Plan 1, Book Problem Solving

Preparing to work (about 5 minutes)

- Take roll if required to do so.
- Have each student take out a sheet of paper and place the usual classroom heading on it—name, and so on.
- Have the students write the topic for the day at the top of their papers: "Book Problem Solving."

Solving problems (about 30 minutes or until the student hands the completed assignment in to you and starts homework)

- Ask the students where they have been working in the textbook.
- Assign an appropriate number of problems to be done in class. (Thirty might be appropriate, but it depends on the type of problems; use your own judgment, but in this case, it is better to assign more than less so that you don't end up with a lot of free time for the kids.)

After each student finishes today's work, it is to be handed in to you, and the student is to start the work that is due at the beginning of the period tomorrow. If a student has not completed today's class work, it is to be collected at the end of the period. Make it clear to students that the problems you have assigned are to be done in class and are not homework. This will keep your students busy and you in control of the classroom.

Start assignment due at the beginning of the period tomorrow.

- Assign more problems from the book, usually about half the number you have assigned in class; use your own judgment. In the case where students have not been issued individual books, tell them to construct and solve the same number of problems that you would have assigned them had they had textbooks to use. *Do not check out books to the class or any student.* If the regular teacher returns to a class where books are missing, you will be less than popular.

Calculators: Some teachers allow them to be used; some do not. Follow what seems to be the usual procedure.

All Grade Levels, Math
Lesson Plan 2, Individual Problem Solving

Preparing to work (about 5 minutes)

- Take roll if required to do so.
- Have each student take out a sheet of paper and place the usual classroom heading on it—name, and so on.
- Have students write the topic for the day at the top of their papers: "Individual Problem Solving."

Giving the instructions for today's assignment (about 5 to 10 minutes)

- Have students *write* all of the following instructions on their papers before starting work:
  1. Multiply the number of your grade level by the number of your grade level (*example:* grade 6 by 6 equals 36).
  2. Add on the age of any member of your family.
  3. Subtract the number of the month in which you were born.
  4. Multiply by 3.
  5. Using A as 1, B as 2, and so on, add the letters in your last name and add on that number.

6. Using the number you have come up with as the answer for each problem you construct, construct twenty problems of the type you have normally been doing in class. Show the steps involved in solving each problem and circle the answer.

7. When you have completed your twenty problems, turn them in to me (the teacher).

Completing today's work (about 30 minutes or until the student hands the completed assignment in to you and starts homework)

After each student finishes today's work, it is to be handed in to you, and the student is to start the work that is due at the beginning of the period tomorrow. If a student has not completed today's class work, it is to be collected at the end of the period. Make it clear to the students that the twenty problems they are to construct and solve are to be done in class and are not homework. This will keep your students busy and you in control of the classroom.

Start the assignment that is due at the beginning of the period tomorrow.

- Tell students: "Double the answer that you have been using and construct ten more problems that are due at the beginning of the period tomorrow. Show the steps involved in solving each problem and circle the answer."

Calculators: Some teachers allow them to be used; some do not. Follow what seems to be the usual procedure.

All Grade Levels, Math
Lesson Plan 3, Partner Problem Solving

Preparing to work (about 5 minutes)

- Take roll if required to do so.
- Have each student take out a sheet of paper and place the usual classroom heading on it—name, and so on.
- Have students write the topic for the day at the top of their papers: "Partner Problem Solving."

Giving instructions for today's assignment (about 5 to 10 minutes)

- Have students *write* all of the following instructions on papers before starting work:
   1. On your paper construct ten problems of the type that you have normally been doing in class. Show the steps involved in solving each problem and circle the answer.

2. When you have completed constructing your ten problems, get together with another student to form a team.

3. The two of you then challenge another team, having them work your problems (without answers) while you work theirs. Keep score on which team solves more problems correctly.

4. Turn your papers in to me (the teacher) when you have finished the game.

Completing today's work (about 30 minutes or until the student hands the completed assignment in to you and starts homework)

After each student finishes today's work, it is to be handed in to you, and the student is to start the work that is due at the beginning of the class tomorrow. If a student has not completed today's class work, it is to be collected at the end of the period. Make it clear to the students that the ten problems they are to construct and solve are to be done in class and are not homework. This will keep your students busy and you in control of the classroom.

Start the assignment that is due at the beginning of the period tomorrow.

- Tell students: "Construct ten more problems that are due at the beginning of the period tomorrow. Show the steps involved in solving each problem and circle the answer."

Calculators: Some teachers allow them to be used; some do not. Follow what seems to be the usual procedure.

All Grade Levels, Math
Lesson Plan 4, Group Problem Solving

Preparing to work (about 5 minutes)

- Take roll if required to do so.
- Have each student take out a sheet of paper and place the usual classroom heading on it—name, and so on.
- Have students write the topic for the day at the top of their papers: "Group Problem Solving."

Giving instructions for today's assignment (about 5 to 10 minutes)

- Have students *write* the following instructions on their papers before starting work:
  1. On your paper construct three problems of the type you have normally been doing in class.

2. Show the steps involved in solving each problem and circle the answer.

3. These problems will be used for a game and then they will be collected at the end of the class.

Constructing the problems (about 10 minutes)

- Each student will be constructing three problems.

Preparing the class to play the problem-solving game

- Divide the class into three teams according to where they are sitting.
- Have each team choose a captain.
- Have each team captain designate:
  - Timekeeper (keeps time)
  - Scorekeeper (keeps score)
  - Verifier (verifies problems and answers)
  - Referee (resolves disputes)

Playing the game

- Have the class do the following as you read each item to them:
  1. Each of the three teams, at the same time, sends a team member to the board to write a problem without giving the answer or showing the steps involved in solving the problem.
  2. Each team, working at their seats, tries to solve the problems presented by the other two teams. Each team comes up with one answer to each problem. There is a limit of 2 minutes total for each team. Time for a team starts when *both* problems have been written on the board. Calculators will not be permitted unless it is some sort of advanced math where calculators are necessary.
  3. *Scoring:* 1 point for each correct answer; subtract 1 point for each incorrect answer.
  4. Repeat process; keep continuing score.
- Five minutes before the end of the class, stop game, collect papers, and assign homework of constructing five more problems that will be due at the beginning of the period tomorrow.

Note: You may call a halt to the game at any time you choose. Add additional problems to homework if you stop the game early.

Chapter Ten

Science Lesson Plans

Grade 6, Science
Noteworthy Scientist, Lesson Plan 1

Preparing to work (about 5 minutes)

- Take roll if required to do so.
- Have each student take out a sheet of paper and place the usual classroom heading on it—name, and so on.
- Have students write the topic for the day at the top of their papers: "George Washington Carver."

Understanding and evaluating information (about 20 minutes)

- Have students *write* the following information on their papers while you make comments (if any) you wish to make:

    A. George Washington Carver was born in Diamond, Missouri, in 1864 and died in 1943.

    B. Carver was an advocate of applying scientific principles to agriculture.

    C. Carver experimented with soil, fertilizer, water, animal feed, human food, and other things to improve crop yields and nutritional value.

    D. Carver discovered over three hundred uses for peanuts.

- Read the following to the students:

    "Born a slave near the end of the Civil War, Carver lost both parents early in life, but was raised by his former owners, who treated him well. Having an early interest and ability in growing plants, Carver, after being graduated from high school at the age of twenty, sought admission to college. After being denied entrance at several colleges because of his race, Carter attended Simpson College and then was able to earn both bachelor's and master's degrees from Iowa Agricultural College. During the many years he taught at Tuskegee Institute, an all-black college in Alabama, Carver worked to improve the lives of poor farmers. Seeing that growing cotton year after year depleted the soil, he came up with many uses for the peanut, thus restoring nitrogen to the soil when farmers grew peanuts instead of cotton."

- Say to the class: "On your papers, evaluate this scientist's contribution to science by using one of the following three labels and explain why you chose that label:

  Not Very Important   Important   Very Important"

Class discussion (about 10 minutes)

- Ask the class: "How important was this scientist's contribution to science and to the world?"

Completing today's assignment (about 10 minutes)

- Have each student write a short paragraph on the same piece of paper he or she has been using. Start with the topic sentence: "George Washington Carver used science to help farmers."

After each student finishes today's work, it is to be handed in to you, and the student is to start the work that is due at the beginning of the period tomorrow.

- Have each student write a short letter to George Washington Carver as if he were still alive.

Grade 6, Science
Noteworthy Scientist, Lesson Plan 2

Preparing to work (about 5 minutes)

- Take roll if required to do so.
- Have each student take out a sheet of paper and place the usual classroom heading on it—name, and so on.
- Have students write the topic for the day at the top of their papers: "Charles Richter."

Understanding and evaluating information (about 20 minutes)

- Have students *write* the following information on their papers while you make comments (if any) you wish to make:

  A. Charles Richter was born in Hamilton, Ohio, in 1900 and died in 1985.

  B. Richter spent his adult life studying earthquakes.

  C. With help from another scientist, he invented the Richter scale.

D. Richter was instrumental in getting Los Angeles to have building codes that limited the height of buildings and took other measures to decrease earthquake damage.

- Read the following to students:

> "Richter was born on a farm in Ohio, and his parents divorced when he was quite young. He grew up in Los Angeles in the care of his grandfather. After earning a Ph.D. in theoretical physics from the California Institute of Technology (Cal Tech), Richter took a job at Cal Tech in the Seismological Laboratory of Pasadena and devoted himself to studying the earth. Working with Beno Gutenberg, the director of the Seismology Laboratory, he invented the Richter scale. It was a vast improvement over the Mercalli scale, an older and less reliable way to measure earthquakes. Richter, while continuing to work at Cal Tech, wrote textbooks, gave lectures, and kept improving the way we study earthquakes. To better understand scientific papers written by scientists who lived in other countries, he learned the languages of Russian, Italian, French, Spanish, and German."

- Say to the class: "On your papers, evaluate this scientist's contribution to science by using one of the following three labels and explain why you chose that label:

Not Very Important   Important   Very Important"

Class discussion (about 10 minutes)

- Ask the class: "How important was this scientist's contribution to science and to the world?"

Completing today's assignment (about 10 minutes)

- Have each student write a short paragraph on the same piece of paper he or she has been using. Start with the topic sentence: "Charles Richter used science to help people have a better chance of surviving earthquakes."

After each student finishes today's work, it is to be handed in to you, and the student is to start the work that is due at the beginning of the period tomorrow.

- Have each student write a short letter to Charles Richter as if he were still alive.

Grade 6, Science
Noteworthy Scientist, Lesson Plan 3

Preparing to work (about 5 minutes)

- Take roll if required to do so.
- Have each student take out a sheet of paper and place the usual classroom heading on it—name, and so on.
- Have students write the topic for the day at the top of their papers: "Alfred Wegener."

Understanding and evaluating information (about 20 minutes)

- Have students *write* the following information on their papers while you make comments (if any) you wish to make:

    A. Alfred Wegener was born in Berlin, Germany, in 1880 and died in 1930.

    B. Wegener believed that the continents were once joined and had drifted apart.

    C. Wegener was the first to propose solid evidence for "continental drift," as it is now called, although he was wrong about what caused it.

    D. Continental drift is now an accepted fact.

- Read the following to students:

    "Wegener received a Ph.D. in astronomy from the University of Berlin in 1905 and soon became involved in weather forecasting. He also studied climates and glaciers. He became a professor of meteorology in 1908. In 1915, he published *The Origin of Continents and Oceans* (English translation). Wegener argued that fossils proved that continents were once joined. If similar fossils were found in similar layers of the earth on different continents, the continents must have been together. Wegener died of a presumed heart attack while leading a scientific expedition in Greenland in 1930. Later, other scientists proved that Wegener was right about the continents and that the Earth's crust is composed of 'plates' that move and change position."

- Say to the class: "On your papers, evaluate this scientist's contribution to science by using one of the following three labels and explain why you chose that label:

    Not Very Important   Important   Very Important"

Class discussion (about 10 minutes)

- Ask the class: "How important was this scientist's contribution to science and to the world?"

Completing today's assignment (about 10 minutes)

- Have each student write a short paragraph on the same piece of paper he or she has been using. Start with the topic sentence: "Alfred Wegener was ridiculed by other scientists during his lifetime for his idea that the continents had been joined."

After each student finishes today's work, it is to be handed in to you, and the student is to start the work that is due at the beginning of the period tomorrow.

- Have each student write a short letter to Alfred Wegener as if he were still alive.

Grade 7, Science
Noteworthy Scientist, Lesson Plan 1

Preparing to work (about 5 minutes)

- Take roll if required to do so.
- Have each student take out a sheet of paper and place the usual classroom heading on it—name, and so on.
- Have students write the topic for the day at the top of their papers: "Louis Pasteur."

Understanding and evaluating information (about 20 minutes)

- Have students *write* the following information on their papers while you make comments (if any) you wish to make:

    A. Louis Pasteur was born in Dole, France, in 1822 and died in 1895.

    B. Pasteur was a founder of microbiology.

    C. Pasteur's studies of microscopic organisms led to his theories about the origin, treatment, and prevention of disease.

    D. In addition to developing the process of pasteurization, Pasteur developed vaccines to prevent cholera, rabies, and anthrax.

- Read the following to students:

    "Pasteur, as a young boy, decided that he would someday become a college professor. In 1847, shortly before his twenty-fifth birthday, he earned his Ph.D. and in 1848 became a professor of chemistry at the University of Strasbourg. After moving to Lille, France, in 1854 to accept a different university teaching job, Pasteur helped a local businessman improve his process of fermentation to produce alcohol. Pasteur concluded that yeast, used in the fermentation process, is a living organism. Pasteur went on to study bacteria and discovered that bacteria can be killed by heat. The process of killing bacteria in liquid with heat became known as 'pasteurization.'"

- Say to the class: "On your papers, evaluate this scientist's contribution to science by using one of the following three labels and explain why you chose that label:

    Not Very Important   Important   Very Important"

Class discussion (about 10 minutes)

- Ask the class: "How important was this scientist's contribution to science and to the world?"

Completing today's assignment (about 10 minutes)

- Have each student write a short paragraph on the same piece of paper he or she has been using. Start with the topic sentence: "Louis Pasteur used science to protect people from disease."

After each student finishes today's work, it is to be handed in to you, and the student is to start the work that is due at the beginning of the period tomorrow.

- Have each student write a short letter to Louis Pasteur as if he were still alive.

Grade 7, Science
Noteworthy Scientist, Lesson Plan 2

Preparing to work (about 5 minutes)

- Take roll if required to do so.
- Have each student take out a sheet of paper and place the usual classroom heading on it—name, and so on.
- Have students write the topic for the day at the top of their papers: "Alice Evans."

Understanding and evaluating information (about 20 minutes)

- Have students write the following information on their papers while you make comments (if any) you wish to make:
    - A. Alice Evans was born in Neath, Pennsylvania, in 1881 and died in 1975.
    - B. Evans discovered that some diseases in cows can be transmitted to humans.
    - C. Evans discovered that brucella bacteria in milk can produce undulant fever in humans who drink the milk.
    - D. Evans led a successful campaign to have milk pasteurized.
- Read the following to students:

    "As a grade school teacher who had never been to college, Evans took a tuition-free, two-year course at Cornell University College of Agriculture that was designed to help teachers teach their students about nature. She went on to the University of Wisconsin and earned a B.A. degree in agriculture and an M.A. in bacteriology. While working for the Wisconsin Agriculture Department's Dairy Division, she began to suspect that drinking cow milk caused humans to have undulant fever characterized by swelling in bone joints, weakness, fever, and pain that kept recurring once contracted. After using guinea pigs to see how brucella bacteria affected them, she documented cases of undulant fever among humans. Convinced that drinking milk from cows that were infected with brucella bacteria caused illness, she crusaded to have milk pasteurized, a process that Louis Pasteur had developed earlier to kill bacteria. Pasteurized milk became the norm in the United States."

- Say to the class: "On your papers, evaluate this scientist's contribution to science by using one of the following three labels and explain why you chose that label:

Not Very Important   Important   Very Important"

Class discussion (about 10 minutes)

- Ask the class: "How important was this scientist's contribution to science and to the world?"

Completing today's assignment (about 10 minutes)

- Have each student write a short paragraph on the same piece of paper he or she has been using. Start with the topic sentence: "Alice Evans used science to protect people from disease."

After each student finishes today's work, it is to be handed in to you, and the student is to start the work that is due at the beginning of the period tomorrow.

- Have each student write a short letter to Alice Evans as if she were still alive.

Grade 7, Science
Noteworthy Scientist, Lesson Plan 3

Preparing to work (about 5 minutes)

- Take roll if required to do so.
- Have each student take out a sheet of paper and place the usual classroom heading on it—name, and so on.
- Have students write the topic for the day at the top of their papers: "Florence Seibert."

Understanding and evaluating information (about 20 minutes)

- Have students *write* the following information on their papers while you make comments (if any) you wish to make:

    A. Florence Seibert was born in Easton, Pennsylvania, in 1897 and died in 1991.

    B. Seibert developed the substance used in the skin test for tuberculosis (TB).

    C. Seibert also discovered that bacteria in distilled water used in intravenous injections caused sudden fevers in patients.

    D. She invented a distilling device to better purify distilled water.

- Read the following to students:

    "At the age of three, Seibert was diagnosed with polio. She was able to overcome the effects of the disease and earned a B.A. from Goucher College in Baltimore, Maryland, in 1918. She received a Ph.D. from Yale University in biochemistry in 1923. While studying for her Ph.D., she invented the distillation device that made distilled water safe for using when injecting proteins into the body. Later, while working at the Henry Phipps Institute that specialized in research and treatment of TB, she built on the scientific discoveries about TB that Robert Koch made years earlier. Seibert developed a substance that could be produced in large enough quantities to administer the TB skin test to millions of people to diagnose and treat the disease in its early stage. The test helped to nearly eradicate the disease in North America and Europe."

- Say to the class: "On your papers, evaluate this scientist's contribution to science by using one of the following three labels and explain why you chose that label:

    Not Very Important   Important   Very Important"

Class discussion (about 10 minutes)

- Ask the class: "How important was this scientist's contribution to science and to the world?"

Completing today's assignment (about 10 minutes)

- Have each student write a short paragraph on the same piece of paper he or she has been using. Start with the topic sentence: "Florence Seibert used science to protect people from disease."

After each student finishes today's work, it is to be handed in to you, and the student is to start the work that is due at the beginning of the period tomorrow.

- Have each student write a short letter to Florence Seibert as if she were still alive.

Grade 8, Science
Noteworthy Scientist, Lesson Plan 1

Preparing to work (about 5 minutes)

- Take roll if required to do so.
- Have each student take out a sheet of paper and place the usual classroom heading on it—name, and so on.
- Have students write the topic for the day at the top of their papers: "Isaac Newton."

Understanding and evaluating information (about 20 minutes)

- Have students *write* the following information on their papers while you make comments (if any) you wish to make:

    A. Isaac Newton was born in Woolsthorpe, Lincolnshire, England, in 1642 and died in 1727.

    B. Newton formulated a set of scientific laws that explained the universe.

    C. Although he is best known for his law of universal gravitation, he formulated other important scientific laws.

    D. His studies of light showed that what we perceive as white light is a mixture of colors that can be split apart.

- Read the following to students:

    "Newton was a premature baby whose father died before he was born. He was not an outstanding student in school, and when he was a teenager his mother removed him from school to work on the farm that he was someday expected to run. Newton, encouraged by his uncle, managed to enter Cambridge University in 1660. Newton earned a B.A. in 1665 and wanted to stay to earn a master's degree. A deadly outbreak of bubonic plague hit London, and Newton returned to the family farm to study on his own. During the time he was studying at home, he began the work on many of the scientific ideas that would make him famous. After returning to the university in 1667, he went on to develop his ideas on how objects move and the effect of gravity on objects. His scientific laws became the basis for understanding and explaining our physical world."

- Say to the class: "On your papers, evaluate this scientist's contribution to science by using one of the following three labels and explain why you chose that label:

    Not Very Important   Important   Very Important"

Class discussion (about 10 minutes)

- Ask the class: "How important was this scientist's contribution to science and to the world?"

Completing today's assignment (about 10 minutes)

- Have each student write a short paragraph on the same piece of paper he or she has been using. Start with the topic sentence: "Isaac Newton changed our view of the world."

After each student finishes today's work, it is to be handed in to you, and the student is to start the work that is due at the beginning of the period tomorrow.

- Have each student write a short letter to Isaac Newton as if he were still alive.

Grade 8, Science
Noteworthy Scientist, Lesson Plan 2

Preparing to work (about 5 minutes)

- Take roll if required to do so.
- Have each student take out a sheet of paper and place the usual classroom heading on it—name, and so on.
- Have students write the topic for the day at the top of their papers: "Robert Goddard."

Understanding and evaluating information (about 20 minutes)

- Have students *write* the following information on their papers while you make comments (if any) you wish to make:
    A. Robert Goddard was born in Worcester, Massachusetts, in 1882 and died in 1945.
    B. Goddard was the first to design liquid-fuel rockets.
    C. Goddard's studies and experiments with rockets laid the groundwork for the rockets that would later propel spacecraft.
    D. Goddard was issued over two hundred patents during his lifetime.
- Read the following to students:

    "Goddard was a very sickly boy who had to drop out of school frequently for his health. He did not enter high school until the age of 19, and at 22, he was the oldest graduating senior the school had ever had. He earned a Ph.D. in physics when he was 29, but he developed tuberculosis and was unable to return to teaching until two years later. Ridiculed by the press as 'Moon Man,' Goddard persisted in experimenting with liquid-fuel rockets. Receiving grants from the Smithsonian Institute and the Guggenheim Foundation, Goddard was eventually able to fly his rockets thousands of feet into the air. The Germans applied Goddard's concepts to weapon development and rained V-2 rockets on England during World War II. Goddard developed the bazooka for the United States. It was used by Americans in World War II to knock out enemy tanks and was the forerunner of rocket-propelled grenades (RPGs)."

- Say to the class: "On your papers, evaluate this scientist's contribution to science by using one of the following three labels and explain why you chose that label:

    Not Very Important   Important   Very Important"

Class discussion (about 10 minutes)

- Ask the class: "How important was this scientist's contribution to science and to the world?"

Completing today's assignment (about 10 minutes)

- Have each student write a short paragraph on the same piece of paper he or she has been using. Start with the topic sentence: "Robert Goddard was ridiculed for his idea that rockets could someday be used to fly people into space."

After each student finishes today's work, it is to be handed in to you, and the student is to start the work that is due at the beginning of the period tomorrow.

- Have each student write a short letter to Robert Goddard as if he were still alive.

Grade 8, Science
Noteworthy Scientist, Lesson Plan 3

Preparing to work (about 5 minutes)

- Take roll if required to do so.
- Have each student take out a sheet of paper and place the usual classroom heading on it—name, and so on.
- Have students write the topic for the day at the top of their papers: "Philo Farnsworth."

Understanding and evaluating information (about 20 minutes)

- Have students write the following information on their papers while you make comments (if any) you wish to make:

A. Philo Farnsworth was born in Indian Creek, Utah, in 1906 and died in 1971.
B. Farnsworth was the inventor of television.
C. Farnsworth designed and built all of the parts for his first television system.
D. Farnsworth made the first cold cathode-ray tube and worked on an early form of radar.

- Read the following to students:

> "Farnsworth came up with the basic design for his television system by the time he was sixteen years old. Fortunately, he showed drawings of his work to his high school chemistry teacher, Justin Tolman. Tolman's testimony would later prove decisive in awarding the patent for television to Farnsworth when Vladimir Zworkin, another inventor, claimed that he had been the first to invent television. In developing his idea for television, Farnsworth was given encouragement by chemistry professors at Brigham Young University and then secured financial backing of $6,000 from investors. In 1927, at the age of twenty-one, Farnsworth was able to transmit a picture, and the following year he made his invention public. Farnsworth and the investors formed a company. Farnsworth went on to work on television and other scientific endeavors."

- Say to the class: "On your papers, evaluate this scientist's contribution to science by using one of the following three labels and explain why you chose that label:

    Not Very Important   Important   Very Important"

Class discussion (about 10 minutes)

- Ask the class: "How important was this scientist's contribution to science and to the world?"

Completing today's assignment (about 10 minutes)

- Have each student write a short paragraph on the same piece of paper he or she has been using. Start with the topic sentence: "Philo Farnsworth used science to change the world."

After each student finishes today's work, it is to be handed in to you, and the student is to start the work that is due at the beginning of the period tomorrow.

- Have each student write a short letter to Philo Farnsworth as if he were still alive.

Grade 9, Science
Noteworthy Scientist, Lesson Plan 1

Preparing to work (about 5 minutes)

- Take roll if required to do so.
- Have each student take out a sheet of paper and place the usual classroom heading on it—name, and so on.
- Have students write the topic for the day at the top of their papers: "Nicolaus Copernicus."

Understanding and evaluating information (about 20 minutes)

- Have students *write* the following information on their papers while you make comments (if any) you wish to make:

  A. Nicolaus Copernicus was born in Torun, Poland, in 1473 and died in 1543.
  B. The Ancient Greek astronomer Ptolemy had said that the Sun revolved around the Earth.
  C. Until Copernicus, Ptolemy's view prevailed.
  D. Copernicus used mathematics to argue that the Earth and other planets revolved around the Sun.

- Read the following to students:

  "Copernicus came from a well-to-do family and was well-educated. He studied church law and was employed by a cathedral. While in Rome to further his studies, he became interested in astronomy after attending a conference on how to reform the calendar. The existing calendar had difficulty conforming to the seasons and the movement of the planets. Copernicus heard about the Ancient Greek astronomer Aristarchus, who had proposed that the Earth revolves around the Sun. Copernicus worked in his spare time for many years to prove that the Earth was not the center of the universe. His book, which ignited a controversy, was published only hours before he died. Copernicus eventually prevailed and Ptolemy lost out."

- Say to the class: "On your papers, evaluate this scientist's contribution to science by using one of the following three labels and explain why you chose that label:

  Not Very Important   Important   Very Important"

Class discussion (about 10 minutes)

- Ask the class: "How important was this scientist's contribution to science and to the world?"

Completing today's assignment (about 10 minutes)

- Have each student write a short paragraph on the same piece of paper he or she has been using. Start with the topic sentence: "It was Copernicus versus Ptolemy in the big science event."

After each student finishes today's work, it is to be handed in to you, and the student is to start the work that is due at the beginning of the period tomorrow.

- Have each student write a short letter to Nicolaus Copernicus as if he were still alive.

Grade 9, Science
Noteworthy Scientist, Lesson Plan 2

Preparing to work (about 5 minutes)

- Take roll if required to do so.
- Have each student take out a sheet of paper and place the usual classroom heading on it—name, and so on.
- Have students write the topic for the day at the top of their papers: "Galileo Galilei."

Understanding and evaluating information (about 20 minutes)

- Have students *write* the following information on their papers while you make comments (if any) you wish to make:

    A. Galileo Galilei was born in Piza, Italy, in 1564 and died in 1642.
    B. Galileo is known to history by his first name.
    C. Galileo made many scientific discoveries.
    D. Galileo, rather than relying on Ancient Greek and Roman Catholic Church authority, used observation, experimentation, and quantitative measurement to reach truth.

- Read the following to students:

    "Although Galileo is probably best known for his discovery that objects of different weights fall at the same rate of speed, he made major contributions in the field of astronomy. Hearing about the invention of the telescope by eyeglass maker Hans Lippershey, Galileo constructed a far superior telescope of his own. Able to magnify at 30 power after he improved it, Galileo investigated the universe, proving the validity of the Copernican theory that the planets revolve around the Sun. He found that the band of light that we call the 'Milky Way' is made up of individual stars. He saw moons revolving around other planets. Galileo used mathematics to calculate distances and movement of heavenly bodies. Forced by the Roman Catholic Church to recant his belief in the Copernican theory, he spent the last few years of his life blind and under house arrest."

- Say to the class: "On your papers, evaluate this scientist's contribution to science by using one of the following three labels and explain why you chose that label:

    Not Very Important   Important   Very Important"

Class discussion (about 10 minutes)

- Ask the class: "How important was this scientist's contribution to science and to the world?"

Completing today's assignment (about 10 minutes)

- Have each student write a short paragraph on the same piece of paper he or she has been using. Start with the topic sentence: "Although Copernicus died before Galileo was born, they were scientific buddies."

After each student finishes today's work, it is to be handed in to you, and the student is to start the work that is due at the beginning of the period tomorrow.

- Have each student write a short letter to Galileo Galilei as if he were still alive.

Grade 9, Science
Noteworthy Scientist, Lesson Plan 3

Preparing to work (about 5 minutes)

- Take roll if required to do so.
- Have each student take out a sheet of paper and place the usual classroom heading on it—name, and so on.
- Have students write the topic for the day at the top of their papers: "Edwin Hubble."

Understanding and evaluating information (about 20 minutes)

- Have students *write* the following information on their papers while you make comments (if any) you wish to make:
    - A. Edwin Hubble was born in Marshfield, Missouri, in 1889 and died in 1953.
    - B. Hubble discovered that there are galaxies other than our own.
    - C. He discovered that the galaxies are speeding away from each other.
    - D. Using Hubble's observations about galaxies, scientists came up with the "Big Bang" theory.
- Read to the class the following:

    "Hubble was an excellent student and athlete in high school, graduating at the age of sixteen. He attended the University of Chicago on an academic scholarship and received his B.A. in math and astronomy in 1910. He went to Oxford on a Rhodes scholarship and returned to the United States in 1913 to practice law. After a short time, he decided he would rather be an astronomer than a lawyer and went to the University of Chicago to study for a Ph.D. in astronomy. After being wounded in World War I while an officer in the U.S. Army, he joined the staff of the Mount Wilson Observatory in Pasadena, California. With powerful telescopes at his disposal, he made his discoveries about galaxies. He also developed a system of classifying galaxies. 'Hubble's Law' states that the farther away a galaxy is from Earth, the faster the galaxy moves away from Earth. When the United States put a powerful telescope into space in 1990, it was named for Hubble, who had died thirty-seven years earlier."

- Say to the class: "On your papers, evaluate this scientist's contribution to science by using one of the following three labels and explain why you chose that label:

Not Very Important   Important   Very Important"

Class discussion (about 10 minutes)

- Ask the class: "How important was this scientist's contribution to science and to the world?"

Completing today's assignment (about 10 minutes)

- Have each student write a short paragraph on the same piece of paper he or she has been using. Start with the topic sentence: "Edwin Hubble was able to see more than a career in law."

After each student finishes today's work, it is to be handed in to you, and the student is to start the work that is due at the beginning of the period tomorrow.

- Have each student write a short letter to Edwin Hubble as if he were still alive.

Grade 10, Science
Noteworthy Scientist, Lesson Plan 1

Preparing to work (about 5 minutes)

- Take roll if required to do so.
- Have each student take out a sheet of paper and place the usual classroom heading on it—name, and so on.
- Have students write the topic for the day at the top of their papers: "Rebecca Craighill Lancefield."

Understanding and evaluating information (about 20 minutes)

- Have students *write* the following information on their papers while you make comments (if any) you wish to make:

   A. Rebecca Craighill Lancefield was born on Staten Island, New York, in 1895 and died in 1981.

   B. Lancefield is noted for her studies of streptococcus bacteria.

   C. She developed a method of classifying (dividing into groups) streptococcus bacteria.

D. The Lancefield System helps medical people identify and treat illnesses caused by streptococcus bacteria.

- Read the following to students:

> "After earning a B.A. in zoology from Wellesley College and an M.A. from Columbia University, where she studied bacteriology, Lancefield went to work at the Rockefeller Institute in New York City. She worked with other scientists investigating a streptococcus outbreak among soldiers. They identified four types of streptococci. While working on her Ph.D. at Columbia, Lancefield found that rheumatic fever was not caused, as some thought, by the alpha-hemolytic class of streptococcus. Throughout her career, she continued to study the streptococcus bacteria, identifying over fifty types. She studied antigens and how they stimulate immune responses. In 1961, she was the first woman elected president of the American Association of Immunologists."

- Say to the class: "On your papers, evaluate this scientist's contribution to science by using one of the following three labels and explain why you chose that label:

Not Very Important   Important   Very Important"

Class discussion (about 10 minutes)

- Ask the class: "How important was this scientist's contribution to science and to the world?"

Completing today's assignment (about 10 minutes)

- Have each student write a short paragraph on the same piece of paper he or she has been using. Start with the topic sentence: "Children owe Rebecca Craighill Lancefield a lot."

After each student finishes today's work, it is to be handed in to you, and the student is to start the work that is due at the beginning of the period tomorrow.

- Have each student write a short letter to Rebecca Craighill Lancefield as if she were still alive.

Grade 10, Science
Noteworthy Scientist, Lesson Plan 2

Preparing to work (about 5 minutes)

- Take roll if required to do so.
- Have each student take out a sheet of paper and place the usual classroom heading on it—name, and so on.

- Have students write the topic for the day at the top of their papers: "Alexander Fleming."

Understanding and evaluating information (about 20 minutes)

- Have students *write* the following information on their papers while you make comments (if any) you wish to make:

  A. Alexander Fleming was born in Lochfield, Scotland, in 1881 and died in 1955.

  B. Fleming discovered penicillin.

  C. Penicillin became known as a "wonder drug" because of its effectiveness in treating diseases caused by bacteria.

  D. The success of penicillin caused researchers to search for and find other antibiotics.

- Read the following to students:

  "Fleming left his family's sheep farm at the age of thirteen and went to London to pursue an education. He was an excellent student and became a medical doctor who preferred medical research rather than having a medical practice. As a military doctor in World War I, Fleming studied infections and decided that some of the antiseptics being used were actually more harmful to white blood cells than to the infections. After the war, Fleming tried to find a substance that would fight harmful bacteria without damaging the body's natural defenses. Accidentally leaving a staphylococcus bacteria culture exposed to air for several days, he noticed mold growing on it. The mold killed the staphylococci it touched. Ten years later, two other scientists overcame the difficulty Fleming had in producing penicillin in large quantities. The three of them shared the Nobel Prize in medicine after penicillin had saved thousands of the wounded in World War II."

- Say to the class: "On your papers, evaluate this scientist's contribution to science by using one of the following three labels and explain why you chose that label:

  Not Very Important   Important   Very Important"

Class discussion (about 10 minutes)

- Ask the class: "How important was this scientist's contribution to science and to the world?"

Completing today's assignment (about 10 minutes)

- Have each student write a short paragraph on the same piece of paper he or she has been using. Start with the topic sentence: "Breakthroughs in science sometimes happen in strange ways."

After each student finishes today's work, it is to be handed in to you, and the student is to start the work that is due at the beginning of the period tomorrow.

- Have each student write a short letter to Alexander Fleming as if he were still alive.

Grade 10, Science
Noteworthy Scientist, Lesson Plan 3

Preparing to work (about 5 minutes)

- Take roll if required to do so.
- Have each student take out a sheet of paper and place the usual classroom heading on it—name, and so on.
- Have students write the topic for the day at the top of their papers: "Charles Drew."

Understanding and evaluating information (about 20 minutes)

- Have students *write* the following information on their papers while you make comments (if any) you wish to make:
  - A. Charles Drew was born in Washington, D.C., in 1904 and died in 1950.
  - B. Drew developed a way to process and store blood plasma.
  - C. In 1940, Drew was the medical supervisor for "Blood for Britain" when Germany was bombing England.
  - D. In 1941, Drew became the director of the American Red Cross Blood Bank in New York City.
- Read the following to students:

  "Drew was graduated from an all-black high school in 1922. He attended Amherst College on an athletic scholarship and later earned a medical degree and a master of surgery degree from McGill University in Canada. In 1938, he accepted a Rockefeller Foundation fellowship to Columbia University to continue the blood research he had begun earlier. Drew found that plasma, the substance remaining when blood cells are removed from blood, could be dehydrated. This meant it could be preserved for quite some time and shipped long distances. The plasma could be used with persons of all blood types because the red cells that determine type had been removed. Battlefield transfusions of plasma saved many lives during World War II. Drew was the first African American to serve on the American Board of Surgery. Drew died from injuries sustained in a car crash in 1950."

- Say to the class: "On your papers, evaluate this scientist's contribution to science by using one of the following three labels and explain why you chose that label:

  Not Very Important   Important   Very Important"

Class discussion (about 10 minutes)

- Ask the class: "How important was this scientist's contribution to science and to the world?"

Completing today's assignment (about 10 minutes)

- Have each student write a short paragraph on the same piece of paper he or she has been using. Start with the topic sentence: "Surgeon Charles Drew saved lives without operating."

After each student finishes today's work, it is to be handed in to you, and the student is to start the work that is due at the beginning of the period tomorrow.

- Have each student write a short letter to Charles Drew as if he were still alive.

Grade 11, Science
Noteworthy Scientist, Lesson Plan 1

Preparing to work (about 5 minutes)

- Take roll if required to do so.
- Have each student take out a sheet of paper and place the usual classroom heading on it—name, and so on.
- Have students write the topic for the day at the top of their papers: "John Dalton."

Understanding and evaluating information (about 20 minutes)

- Have students *write* the following information on their papers while you make comments (if any) you wish to make:
  - A. John Dalton was born in Eaglesfield, Cumberland, England, in 1766 and died in 1844.
  - B. Dalton assigned atomic weights to elements.
  - C. Although some of the words were different, Dalton expressed the ideas of atoms, molecules, elements, and chemical compounds.
  - D. Dalton's classification of elements by atomic weights laid the basis for modern chemistry.
- Read the following to students:

  "The idea of things being composed of atoms went back at least to the Ancient Greek, Democritus, but not until the time of John Dalton, over 2,000 years later, did the theory gain acceptance. Dalton, from a poor family, dropped out of school by the age of eleven. A bright boy, he became a tutor of younger children and a teacher at twelve. He made little money at it and worked on local farms. At fifteen he was hired to teach elementary school. He remained a tutor and teacher the rest of his life. Mostly self-taught, he began investigating scientific things that interested him. He listened to lectures of well-known scientists whenever possible and began writing scientific papers. In 1808, his book *New Systems of Chemical Philosophy* was published, and his idea about atomic weights was soon accepted by other scientists."

- Say to the class: "On your papers, evaluate this scientist's contribution to science by using one of the following three labels and explain why you chose that label:

Not Very Important   Important   Very Important"

Class discussion (about 10 minutes)

- Ask the class: "How important was this scientist's contribution to science and to the world?"

Completing today's assignment (about 10 minutes)

- Have each student write a short paragraph on the same piece of paper he or she has been using. Start with the topic sentence: "Lack of formal education did not stop John Dalton from learning."

After each student finishes today's work, it is to be handed in to you, and the student is to start the work that is due at the beginning of the period tomorrow.

- Have each student write a short letter to John Dalton as if he were still alive.

Grade 11, Science
Noteworthy Scientist, Lesson Plan 2

Preparing to work (about 5 minutes)

- Take roll if required to do so.
- Have each student take out a sheet of paper and place the usual classroom heading on it—name, and so on.
- Have students write the topic for the day at the top of their papers: "Wilhelm Röntgen."

Understanding and evaluating information (about 20 minutes)

- Have students *write* the following information on their papers while you make comments (if any) you wish to make:
    A. Wilhelm Röntgen was born in Lennep, Germany, in 1845 and died in 1923.
    B. Röntgen discovered X rays.

C. X rays were quickly adapted to medical use.

D. The discovery of X rays led to important discoveries by other scientists.

- Read the following to students:

> "Röntgen was expelled from school at about the age of seventeen, accused of drawing an unflattering picture of his teacher. He managed to get his education back on track by going to other schools and earned a doctor's degree in 1869. For the next few years he worked as an assistant to one of his college professors until he himself was appointed a professor of physics. In 1895, while doing an experiment with cathode rays, Röntgen had darkened his laboratory and covered a cathode-ray tube with black paper. When he turned on the tube, mysterious rays, which he later called X rays, caused a nearby screen covered with barium plantinocyanide to light up. He continued to experiment with X rays. It is believed that the first X ray photo ever made was of his wife's hand. In 1901, Röntgen was awarded the first Nobel Peace Prize in physics."

- Say to the class: "On your papers, evaluate this scientist's contribution to science by using one of the following three labels and explain why you chose that label:

  Not Very Important   Important   Very Important"

Class discussion (about 10 minutes)

- Ask the class: "How important was this scientist's contribution to science and to the world?"

Completing today's assignment (about 10 minutes)

- Have each student write a short paragraph on the same piece of paper he or she has been using. Start with the topic sentence: "Wilhelm Röntgen changed the way medicine was practiced."

After each student finishes today's work, it is to be handed in to you, and the student is to start the work that is due at the beginning of the period tomorrow.

- Have each student write a short letter to Wilhelm Röntgen as if he were still alive.

Grade 11, Science
Noteworthy Scientist, Lesson Plan 3

Preparing to work (about 5 minutes)

- Take roll if required to do so.
- Have each student take out a sheet of paper and place the usual classroom heading on it—name, and so on.
- Have students write the topic for the day at the top of their papers: "Marie Curie."

Understanding and evaluating information (about 20 minutes)

- Have students *write* the following information on their papers while you make comments (if any) you wish to make:
    A. Marie Curie was born in Warsaw, Poland, in 1867 and died in 1934.
    B. Marie, along with her husband, Pierre, investigated and developed knowledge about radioactivity.
    C. The Curies discovered two radioactive elements, polonium and radium.
    D. After her husband's death, Marie continued to work with radium and raised money for its use in the diagnosis and treatment of disease.
- Read the following to students:

    "Marie's Polish name was Marya Sklodowska, but she changed it to the French 'Marie' when she went to study in France. Later, she became 'Madame Curie' when she married Pierre Curie. Pierre was already a well-known scientist at the time of the wedding, but Marie, who was brilliant in her own right, eventually earned a Ph.D. Although French physicist Henri Becquerel discovered radioactivity, Pierre and Marie studied and experimented with it. The three of them shared the Nobel Prize in physics in 1903. Marie earned a second Nobel Prize in 1911, which was in chemistry for her continuing work on polonium and radium. Pierre did not share in the second prize, having been run over and killed by a horse-drawn wagon on a Paris street in 1906."

- Say to the class: "On your papers, evaluate this scientist's contribution to science by using one of the following three labels and explain why you chose that label:

    Not Very Important   Important   Very Important"

Class discussion (about 10 minutes)

- Ask the class: "How important was this scientist's contribution to science and to the world?"

Completing today's assignment (about 10 minutes)

- Have each student write a short paragraph on the same piece of paper he or she has been using. Start with the topic sentence: "Marie Curie died of a radiation-related illness, but her research led to medical treatment that saves many people today."

After each student finishes today's work, it is to be handed in to you, and the student is to start the work that is due at the beginning of the period tomorrow.

- Have each student write a short letter to Marie Curie as if she were still alive.

Grade 12, Science
Noteworthy Scientist, Lesson Plan 1

Preparing to work (about 5 minutes)

- Take roll if required to do so.
- Have each student take out a sheet of paper and place the usual classroom heading on it—name, and so on.
- Have students write the topic for the day at the top of their papers: "Nikola Tesla."

Understanding and evaluating information (about 20 minutes)

- Have students *write* the following information on their papers while you make comments (if any) you wish to make:
    - A. Nikola Tesla was born in Smiljan, Croatia, in 1856 and died in 1943.
    - B. Tesla developed alternating electrical current (AC), wherein electrons move in one direction and then the other.
    - C. Thomas Edison committed himself to direct electrical current (DC), electrons always moving in the same direction.
    - D. AC became the method of supplying the world with electricity.
- Read the following to students:

    "Tesla's early schooling took place in his native Croatia. While attending a technical school in Austria and then a university in Czechoslovakia, Tesla developed an interest in electricity. In 1884, he moved to the United States and began working at Thomas Edison's research laboratory. He only worked for Edison for a year, as the two disagreed about, among other things, the best way to transmit electricity. Tesla acquired over a hundred patents during his lifetime, but perhaps his greatest achievement was designing the world's first hydroelectric generating plant, which was located at Niagara Falls and used the AC system. Many of Tesla's scientific ideas were ahead of his time and did not receive serious attention until after his death."

- Say to the class: "On your papers, evaluate this scientist's contribution to science by using one of the following three labels and explain why you chose that label:

    Not Very Important   Important   Very Important"

Class discussion (about 10 minutes)

- Ask the class: "How important was this scientist's contribution to science and to the world?"

Completing today's assignment (about 10 minutes)

- Have each student write a short paragraph on the same piece of paper he or she has been using. Start with the topic sentence: "Nikola Tesla still shines brightly."

After each student finishes today's work, it is to be handed in to you, and the student is to start the work that is due at the beginning of the period tomorrow.

- Have each student write a short letter to Nikola Tesla as if he were still alive.

Grade 12, Science
Noteworthy Scientist, Lesson Plan 2

Preparing to work (about 5 minutes)

- Take roll if required to do so.
- Have each student take out a sheet of paper and place the usual classroom heading on it—name, and so on.
- Have students write the topic for the day at the top of their papers: "Enrico Fermi."

Understanding and evaluating information (about 20 minutes)

- Have students *write* the following information on their papers while you make comments (if any) you wish to make:
  A. Enrico Fermi was born in Rome, Italy, in 1901 and died in 1954.
  B. Fermi did research on having neutrons penetrate the nucleus of an atom.
  C. By bombarding the nucleus of an atom with neutrons, scientists could sometimes split the atom apart and release energy.
  D. Fermi was a key figure in producing the atomic bomb.
- Read the following to students:

  "Fermi, a brilliant student, earned a Ph.D. in physics at the age of twenty-one. While teaching at the University of Florence, Fermi conducted experiments having neutrons penetrate the nuclei of atoms of various elements. This eventually led to nuclear fission, the splitting of atoms and the release of energy. When Fermi went to Sweden in 1938 to accept the Nobel Prize in physics, he did not return to Italy. He took his Jewish wife to the United

States to escape the Fascists' persecution of Jews. Fermi taught at Columbia University and then joined the secret Manhattan Project. Fermi led the group that produced the world's first nuclear reactor that split apart uranium atoms and created a continuing reaction of splitting atoms. The chain reaction made the atomic bomb possible. Nuclear reactors later led to nuclear submarines, nuclear power plants, and other applications of nuclear fission."

- Say to the class: "On your papers, evaluate this scientist's contribution to science by using one of the following three labels and explain why you chose that label:

Not Very Important   Important   Very Important"

Class discussion (about 10 minutes)

- Ask the class: "How important was this scientist's contribution to science and to the world?"

Completing today's assignment (about 10 minutes)

- Have each student write a short paragraph on the same piece of paper he or she has been using. Start with the topic sentence: "Enrico Fermi brought in the atomic age."

After each student finishes today's work, it is to be handed in to you, and the student is to start the work that is due at the beginning of the period tomorrow.

- Have each student write a short letter to Enrico Fermi as if he were still alive.

Grade 12, Science
Noteworthy Scientist, Lesson Plan 3

Preparing to work (about 5 minutes)

- Take roll if required to do so.
- Have each student take out a sheet of paper and place the usual classroom heading on it—name, and so on.
- Have students write the topic for the day at the top of their papers: "Luis Alvarez."

Understanding and evaluating information (about 20 minutes)

- Have students *write* the following information on their papers while you make comments (if any) you wish to make:
    - A. Luis Alvarez was born in San Francisco, California, in 1911 and died in 1988.
    - B. Alvarez made contributions to science in many areas.

C. He was awarded the Nobel Prize for physics in 1968 for his work on bubble chambers and subatomic particles.

D. He and his son Walter came up with the theory that a giant asteroid hitting the Earth had caused the demise of the dinosaurs.

- Read the following to students:

> "Alvarez earned his physics degrees, B.A., M.A., and Ph.D., at the University of Chicago and became a research scientist at the University of California at Berkeley. Alvarez quickly began making discoveries and contributing to scientific projects. The wavelength of light from a mercury vapor lamp he and a student made became the official standard length used by the U.S. Bureau of Standards. Tritium, a radioactive isotope of hydrogen, was discovered by Alvarez. Alvarez went to work at the Massachusetts Institute of Technology and helped develop three types of radar systems that the United States used in World War II. While working at Los Alamos, New Mexico, he helped develop the detonating device for the atomic bomb. Returning to Berkeley after the war, he worked on particle physics, developing particle accelerators and bubble chambers, devices that had already been invented by others to study the smallest particles of atoms, but were vastly improved by Alvarez. In 1980, Alvarez and his son, a geologist, ignited a scientific controversy with their theory of an asteroid causing the extinction of dinosaurs."

- Say to the class: "On your papers, evaluate this scientist's contribution to science by using one of the following three labels and explain why you chose that label:

Not Very Important   Important   Very Important"

Class discussion (about 10 minutes)

- Ask the class: "How important was this scientist's contribution to science and to the world?"

Completing today's assignment (about 10 minutes)

- Have each student write a short paragraph on the same piece of paper he or she has been using. Start with the topic sentence: "Luis Alvarez was a very talented scientist."

After each student finishes today's work, it is to be handed in to you, and the student is to start the work that is due at the beginning of the period tomorrow.

- Have each student write a short letter to Luis Alvarez as if he were still alive.

Chapter Eleven

Social Studies Lesson Plans

Grade 6, Social Studies
U.S. Geography, Lesson Plan 1

Preparing to work (about 5 minutes)

- Take roll if required to do so.
- Have each student take out a sheet of paper and place the usual classroom heading on it—name, and so on.
- Have students write the topic for the day at the top of their papers: "Coastal Areas."

Understanding and applying basic facts (about 20 minutes)

- Have students *write* the following facts on their papers while you make any relevant comments you choose to make that will clarify the facts:
  - A. The Continental United States has three major coastal areas: the East Coast, the West Coast, and the Gulf Coast.
  - B. The East Coast, bordered by the Atlantic Ocean, extends from Maine to Florida.
  - C. The West Coast, bordered by the Pacific Ocean, extends from the state of Washington to California.
  - D. The Gulf Coast, bordered by the Gulf of Mexico, extends from Florida to Texas.
- Have students number from 1 to 10 on their papers and guess the location for each item you read by *writing* East Coast, West Coast, or Gulf Coast. After students have responded to all ten, read the correct answers:
  - 1. New York
  - 2. Los Angeles
  - 3. Mouth of the Mississippi

  - 1. East Coast
  - 2. West Coast
  - 3. Gulf Coast

4. New Orleans	4. Gulf Coast
5. Coldest in winter	5. East Coast (Maine)
6. Hottest in winter	6. East Coast (Florida)
7. Rainy winters and dry summers	7. West Coast (Southern California)
8. The most clouds, fog, rain, drizzle, in winter	8. West Coast (Washington, Oregon)
9. Outer Banks	9. East Coast
10. Galveston	10. Gulf Coast

Class discussion (about 10 minutes)

- Say to the class: "Both Florida and California attract a lot of people because of their warm climates. Which would be the better place to live and why do you think so?"

Completing today's assignment (about 10 minutes)

- Have each student write a short paragraph on the same piece of paper he or she has been using. Start with the topic sentence: "Coastal cities have been and are very important to the United States."

After each student finishes today's work, it is to be handed in to you, and the student is to start the work that is due at the beginning of the period tomorrow.

- Have each student label three columns on a new sheet of paper and list five things he or she thinks might fit each column. An example is given:

East Coast	*West Coast*	*Gulf Coast*
1. Borders Atlantic	1. Borders Pacific	1. Borders Gulf of Mexico

Grade 6, Social Studies
U.S. Geography, Lesson Plan 2

Preparing to work (about 5 minutes)

- Take roll if required to do so.
- Have each student take out a sheet of paper and place the usual classroom heading on it—name, and so on.
- Have students write the topic for the day at the top of their papers: "The Interior."

Understanding and applying basic facts (about 20 minutes)

- Have students *write* the following facts on their papers while you make any relevant comments you choose to make that will clarify the facts:

    A. Four important mountain areas in the United States are the Appalachian Highlands, the Rocky Mountains, the Sierra Nevada, and the Cascade Mountains.

    B. Four important rivers in the United States are the Missouri, the Mississippi, the Colorado, and the Tennessee.

    C. There are five Great Lakes: Superior, Michigan, Huron, Ontario, and Erie.

    D. The large area of grassland in the center of the United States is called "The Great Plains."

- Have students number from 1 to 10 on their papers and guess by *writing* Lake(s), Mountain(s), River(s), or Plain(s) for each item you read. After students have responded to all ten, read the correct answers:

1.	Kansas wheat field	1.	Plains
2.	Continental Divide	2.	Mountains
3.	Hoover Dam	3.	River (or manmade lake)
4.	Texas cattle ranch	4.	Plains
5.	Columbia	5.	River
6.	Timberline	6.	Mountains
7.	Grand Coulee Dam	7.	River (or manmade lake)
8.	Tennessee Valley Authority (TVA)	8.	River (or manmade lakes)
9.	Great Salt	9.	Lake
10.	Barge hauling iron ore to Chicago	10.	Lakes

Class discussion (about 10 minutes)

- Ask the class: "Would it make any difference if the Rocky Mountains extended east and west instead of north and south?"

Completing today's assignment (about 10 minutes)

- Have each student write a short paragraph on the same piece of paper he or she has been using. Start with the topic sentence: "Rivers have many uses."

After each student finishes today's work, it is to be handed in to you, and the student is to start the work that is due at the beginning of the period tomorrow.

- Have each student label three columns on a new sheet of paper and list five things he or she thinks might fit each column. An example is given:

Rivers	*Mountains*	*Plains*
1. Used for electricity	1. Source of many rivers	1. Good for crops

Grade 6, Social Studies
U.S. Geography, Lesson Plan 3

Preparing to work (about 5 minutes)

- Take roll if required to do so.
- Have each student take out a sheet of paper and place the usual classroom heading on it—name, and so on.
- Have students write the topic for the day at the top of their papers: "Alaska and Hawaii."

Understanding and applying basic facts (about 20 minutes)

- Have students *write* the following facts on their papers while you make any relevant comments you choose to make that will clarify the facts:
  - A. Alaska became the forty-ninth state on January 3, 1959. Hawaii became the fiftieth state on August 21, 1959.
  - B. The United States purchased Alaska from Russia in 1867. Hawaii was annexed by the United States in 1898.
  - C. Alaska, the largest U.S. state, has been important because of oil, mineral wealth, wildlife, forests, tourism, and national defense.
  - D. The eight main islands and many smaller islands of Hawaii are the tops of ancient volcanoes. Hawaii has been important because of its location, agriculture, tourism, and national defense.
- Have students number from 1 to 10 on their papers and guess by *writing* Alaska or Hawaii for each item you read. After students have responded to all ten, read the correct answers:

1. Honolulu	1. Hawaii
2. Rainiest place on Earth	2. Hawaii (Mt. Waialeale)
3. Juneau	3. Alaska
4. Highest mountain in United States	4. Alaska (Mt. McKinley)
5. Pearl Harbor	5. Hawaii
6. Long winter nights	6. Alaska
7. Gold Rush in late 1800s	7. Alaska
8. Pineapple growers	8. Hawaii
9. Polynesian heritage	9. Hawaii
10. Aleut and Inuit heritage	10. Alaska

Class discussion (about 10 minutes)

- Ask the class: "Which is likely to be more important to the United States in the future, Alaska or Hawaii?"

Completing today's assignment (about 10 minutes)

- Have each student write a short paragraph on the same piece of paper he or she has been using. Start with the topic sentence: "Alaska and Hawaii are both very valuable to the United States."

After each student finishes today's work, it is to be handed in to you, and the student is to start the work that is due at the beginning of the period tomorrow.

- Have each student label two columns on a new sheet of paper and list ten things he or she thinks might fit each column. An example is given:

Alaska

1. Snows a lot

Hawaii

1. Rains a lot

Grade 7, Social Studies
World Geography, Lesson Plan 1

Preparing to work (about 5 minutes)

- Take roll if required to do so.
- Have each student take out a sheet of paper and place the usual classroom heading on it—name, and so on.
- Have students write the topic for the day at the top of their papers: "Continents."

Understanding and applying basic facts (about 20 minutes)

- Have students *write* the following facts on their papers while you make any relevant comments you choose to make that will clarify the facts:
    A. There are seven continents on Earth: Asia, Africa, North America, South America, Antarctica, Europe, and Australia.
    B. Less than a third of the surface of the Earth is covered by land.
    C. Small bodies of land surrounded by water are called "islands," not continents.
    D. Most of the land area of the Earth is located north of the equator.
- Have students number from 1 to 10 on their papers and guess by *writing* the name of a continent for each item you read. After students have responded to all ten, read the correct answers:

    1. Largest continent
    2. Smallest continent
    3. Largest population
    4. Smallest population
    5. Highest mountain
    6. Dead Sea

    1. Asia
    2. Australia
    3. Asia
    4. Antarctica
    5. Asia (Mt. Everest)
    6. Asia

7. Alps	7. Europe
8. Largest desert	8. Africa (Sahara)
9. Amazon River	9. South America
10. Mount McKinley	10. North America

Class discussion (about 10 minutes)

- Say to the class: "Thinking of the Earth as a round ball, where do you think most of the people live and why might this be?"

Completing today's assignment (about 10 minutes)

- Have each student write a short paragraph on the same piece of paper he or she has been using. Start with the topic sentence: "There are seven continents on Earth."

After each student finishes today's work, it is to be handed in to you, and the student is to start the work that is due at the beginning of the period tomorrow.

- Have each student label three columns on a new sheet of paper and list five things he or she thinks might fit each column. An example is given:

Asia	*Europe*	*Africa*
1. Most people	1. Located next to Asia	1. Equator crosses it

Grade 7, Social Studies
World Geography, Lesson Plan 2

Preparing to work (about 5 minutes)

- Take roll if required to do so.
- Have each student take out a sheet of paper and place the usual classroom heading on it—name, and so on.
- Have students write the topic for the day at the top of their papers: "Oceans."

Understanding and applying basic facts (about 20 minutes)

- Have students *write* the following facts on their papers while you make any relevant comments you choose to make that will clarify the facts:
    A. More than two-thirds of the Earth are covered by water.
    B. Large bodies of water are called "oceans." Bodies of water smaller than oceans are called "seas."
    C. The four oceans on Earth are the Pacific, Atlantic, Indian, and Arctic.
    D. The equator crosses all of the oceans except the Arctic.

- Have students number from 1 to 10 on their papers and guess by *writing* the name of an ocean for each item you read. After students have responded to all ten, read the correct answers:

1.	North Pole	1.	Arctic
2.	Between Europe and North America	2.	Atlantic
3.	Between Africa and South America	3.	Atlantic
4.	Between Asia and North America	4.	Pacific
5.	Between Africa and Australia	5.	Indian
6.	Largest ocean	6.	Pacific
7.	Second-largest ocean	7.	Atlantic
8.	Hawaii	8.	Pacific
9.	Mostly frozen	9.	Arctic
10.	Touches Arabian Sea	10.	Indian

Class discussion (about 10 minutes)

- Say to the class: "Name some countries that are composed entirely of islands and suggest how they might have been affected by the ocean."

Completing today's assignment (about 10 minutes)

- Have each student write a short paragraph on the same piece of paper he or she has been using. Start with the topic sentence: "Although we live on land, the Earth is mainly water."

After each student finishes today's work, it is to be handed in to you, and the student is to start the work that is due at the beginning of the period tomorrow.

- Have each student label three columns on a new sheet of paper and list five things he or she thinks might fit each column. An example is given:

Pacific	*Atlantic*	*Indian*
1. Largest ocean	1. <u>Titanic</u> sank	1. South of India

Grade 7, Social Studies
World Geography, Lesson Plan 3

Preparing to work (about 5 minutes)

- Take roll if required to do so.
- Have each student take out a sheet of paper and place the usual classroom heading on it—name, and so on.
- Have students write the topic for the day at the top of their papers: "Climates."

Understanding and applying basic facts (about 20 minutes)

- Have students write the following facts on their papers while you make any relevant comments you choose to make that will clarify the facts:

    A. Climates are affected by a number of things; among them are distance from the sun, elevation, bodies of water, mountains, rainfall, and wind.

    B. In general, the closer to the equator (low latitudes), the hotter the climate.

    C. In general, the farther away from the equator (high latitudes), the colder the climate.

    D. In general, places quite a way from the equator and quite a way from the Poles (mid latitudes), have the most liveable climates.

- Have students number from 1 to 10 on their papers and guess by writing Low latitude, Mid latitude, or High latitude for each item you read. After students have responded to all ten, read the correct answers:

1.	United States	1.	Mid latitude
2.	France	2.	Mid latitude
3.	China	3.	Mid latitude
4.	Panama	4.	Low latitude
5.	Uganda	5.	Low latitude
6.	Top of Alaska	6.	High latitude
7.	Greenland	7.	High latitude
8.	South Africa	8.	Mid latitude
9.	Indonesia	9.	Low latitude
10.	Antarctica	10.	High latitude

Class discussion (about 10 minutes)

- Ask the class: "Why are the winter temperatures of Portland, Oregon, warmer than the winter temperatures of Minneapolis, Minnesota, even though Minneapolis is closer to the equator?"

Completing today's assignment (about 10 minutes)

- Have each student write a short paragraph on the same piece of paper he or she has been using. Start with the topic sentence: "People do many things to adjust to the climate where they live."

After each student finishes today's work, it is to be handed in to you, and the student is to start the work that is due at the beginning of the period tomorrow.

- Have each student label three columns on a new sheet of paper and list five things he or she thinks might fit each column. An example is given:

Low Latitude	*Mid Latitude*	*High Latitude*
1. Usually very hot	1. May be hot, cold, or both	1. Usually cold

Grade 8, Social Studies
American History, Lesson Plan 1

Preparing to work (about 5 minutes)

- Take roll if required to do so.
- Have each student take out a sheet of paper and place the usual classroom heading on it—name, and so on.
- Have students write the topic for the day at the top of their papers: "Explorers and Settlers Before 1800."

Understanding and applying basic facts (about 20 minutes)

- Have students *write* the following facts on their papers while you make any relevant comments you choose to make that will clarify the facts:
    - A. Many tribes of Native Americans lived in North America before the arrival of the Europeans.
    - B. The Dutch, English, French, and Spanish took the lead in exploring and settling North America.
    - C. The Vikings probably arrived centuries before Columbus, but they did not stay.
    - D. The Swedes settled what later became Delaware. The Russians settled Alaska and explored south along the coast.
- Have students number from 1 to 10 on their papers and guess by *writing* England, France, or Spain for each item you read. After students have responded to all ten, read the correct answers:

    1. Explored Florida   1. Spain
    2. Settled Jamestown   2. England
    3. Settled Quebec   3. France
    4. Settled St. Augustine   4. Spain
    5. Settled Santa Fe   5. Spain
    6. Settled East Coast, became a part of the United States   6. England
    7. Settled Southwest, a part of Mexico and now United States 7. Spain
    8. Explored the Mississippi River and settled New Orleans   8. France
    9. Early settlements in Canada   9. France
    10. The Thirteen Colonies   10. England

Class discussion (about 10 minutes)

- Ask the class: "Why were large areas of North America called New Spain, New England, and New France? What eventually happened to each of those areas?"

Completing today's assignment (about 10 minutes)

- Have each student write a short paragraph on the same piece of paper he or she has been using. Start with the topic sentence: "'E pluribus unum' means 'one out of many' and that is why this Latin phrase is on the back of dollar bills."

After each student finishes today's work, it is to be handed in to you, and the student is to start the work that is due at the beginning of the period tomorrow.

- Have each student label three columns on a new sheet of paper and list five things he or she thinks might fit each column. An example is given:

England	*France*	*Spain*
1. Thirteen Colonies	1. Settled Canada	1. Settled the Southwest

Grade 8, Social Studies
American History, Lesson Plan 2

Preparing to work (about 5 minutes)

- Take roll if required to do so.
- Have each student take out a sheet of paper and place the usual classroom heading on it—name, and so on.
- Have students write the topic for the day at the top of their papers: "Going West in the 1800s."

Understanding and applying basic facts (about 20 minutes)

- Have students *write* the following facts on their papers while you make any relevant comments you choose to make that will clarify the facts:
  - A. From the original Thirteen Colonies the United States expanded west across the continent.
  - B. Explorers, hunters, trappers, fur traders, and "Mountain Men" led the way west.
  - C. Missionaries, miners, cattle ranchers, railroad builders, and settlers went west.
  - D. There was often conflict, which resulted in a series of battles between the U.S. Army and Native Americans.
- Have students number from 1 to 10 on their papers and guess by *writing* Mining, Ranching, or Farming as the main reason most Easterners were initially attracted to a particular place that you read. After students have responded to all ten, read the correct answers:

1. Texas	1. Ranching
2. Colorado	2. Mining
3. Nevada	3. Mining

<table>
<tr><td>4.</td><td>Nebraska</td><td>4.</td><td>Farming</td></tr>
</table>

4.	Nebraska	4.	Farming
5.	South Dakota	5.	Mining
6.	California	6.	Mining
7.	Iowa	7.	Farming
8.	Oregon	8.	Farming
9.	Wyoming	9.	Ranching
10.	Missouri	10.	Farming

Class discussion (about 10 minutes)

- Ask the class: "Was Brigham Young successful when he lead the Mormons west to the Great Salt Lake to establish a religious settlement where Mormons would be free to live the way they wanted to live?"

Completing today's assignment (about 10 minutes)

- Have each student write a short paragraph on the same piece of paper he or she has been using. Start with the topic sentence: "There were many reasons Easterners wanted to go west."

After each student finishes today's work, it is to be handed in to you, and the student is to start the work that is due at the beginning of the period tomorrow.

- Have each student label three columns on a new sheet of paper and list five things he or she thinks might fit each column. An example is given:

Settlers	*Native Americans*	*U.S. Army*
1. Wanted land	1. Wanted to keep land	1. Protected settlers

Grade 8, Social Studies
American History, Lesson Plan 3

Preparing to work (about 5 minutes)

- Take roll if required to do so.
- Have each student take out a sheet of paper and place the usual classroom heading on it—name, and so on.
- Have students write the topic for the day at the top of their papers: "The U.S. Is a World Power."

Understanding and applying basic facts (about 20 minutes)

- Have students *write* the following facts on their papers while you make any relevant comments you choose to make that will clarify the facts:

A. After the Civil War (1861–1865) the United States went through a period of rapid industrialization (factories).

B. After the Civil War the United States went through a continuing period of immigration (people coming here).

C. After the Civil War the United States went through a continuing period of urbanization (growth of cities).

D. As the twentieth century began, the United States was becoming a world power. By the end of the twentieth century, the United States was called by some "the only superpower."

- Have students number from 1 to 10 on their papers and guess by *writing* Industrialization, Immigration, or Urbanization for each item you read. After the students have responded to all ten, read the correct answers:

1. Standard Oil		1. Industrialization
2. Ellis Island		2. Immigration
3. Statue of Liberty		3. Immigration
4. U.S. Steel		4. Industrialization
5. Skyscrapers		5. Urbanization
6. Ethnic neighborhoods		6. Urbanization
7. Labor unions		7. Industrialization
8. Suburbs		8. Urbanization
9. Irish potato famine		9. Immigration
10. Henry Ford		10. Industrialization

Class discussion (about 10 minutes)

- Ask the class: "Will the United States keep its position of leadership throughout the twenty-first century?"

Completing today's assignment (about 10 minutes)

- Have each student write a short paragraph on the same piece of paper he or she has been using. Start with the topic sentence: "Although there are approximately 190 countries in the world, I live in the United States."

After each student finishes today's work, it is to be handed in to you, and the student is to start the work that is due at the beginning of the period tomorrow.

- Have each student label three columns on a new sheet of paper and list five things he or she thinks might fit each column. An example is given:

Industrialization	*Immigration*	*Urbanization*
1. More products	1. New people	1. Skyscrapers

Grade 9, Social Studies
American Government, Lesson Plan 1

Preparing to work (about 5 minutes)

- Take roll if required to do so.
- Have each student take out a sheet of paper and place the usual classroom heading on it—name, and so on.
- Have students write the topic for the day at the top of their papers: "The Constitution of the United States."

Understanding and applying basic facts (about 20 minutes)

- Have students *write* the following facts on their papers while you make any relevant comments you choose to make that will clarify the facts:
    A. The Constitution of the United States is the basic plan for our government.
    B. The Constitution of the United States was written in 1787 and adopted in 1789.
    C. The Constitution consists of a Preamble, Articles, and Amendments.
    D. The Preamble starts the Constitution. The Articles are the original parts of the Constitution. The Amendments are the changes to the Constitution.
- Have students number from 1 to 10 on their papers and guess by *writing* Preamble, Article, or Amendment for each item you read. After students have responded to all ten, read them the correct answers:

    1. No slavery
    2. We the people
    3. Congress shall have the power
    4. Creates a president
    5. Women's right to vote
    6. No legal alcohol
    7. Alcohol is again legal
    8. Secure the blessings of liberty
    9. Creates the Supreme Court
    10. Creates an income tax

    1. Amendment
    2. Preamble
    3. Article
    4. Article
    5. Amendment
    6. Amendment
    7. Amendment
    8. Preamble
    9. Article
    10. Amendment

Class discussion (about 10 minutes)

- Ask the class: "Why was it necessary to have amendments (changes) to the original Constitution, and what are some of the important changes?"

Completing today's assignment (about 10 minutes)

- Have each student write a short paragraph on the same piece of paper he or she has been using. Start with the topic sentence: "The U.S. Constitution is a very important document."

After each student finishes today's work, it is to be handed in to you, and the student is to start the work that is due at the beginning of the period tomorrow.

- Have each student label three columns on a new sheet of paper and list five things he or she thinks might fit each column. An example is given:

Preamble	*Articles*	*Amendments*
1. Blessings of liberty	1. Created Congress	1. No slavery

Grade 9, Social Studies
American Government, Lesson Plan 2

Preparing to work (about 5 minutes)

- Take roll if required to do so.
- Have each student take out a sheet of paper and place the usual classroom heading on it—name, and so on.
- Have students write the topic for the day at the top of their papers: "The Government of the United States."

Understanding and applying basic facts (about 20 minutes)

- Have students *write* the following facts on their papers while you make any relevant comments you choose to make that will clarify the facts:
    A. The government of the United States is divided into three parts: Legislative, Executive, and Judicial.
    B. The legislative branch passes laws.
    C. The executive branch executes (carries out/administers) the laws.
    D. The judicial branch interprets the laws.
- Have students number from 1 to 10 on their papers and guess by *writing* Legislative, Executive, or Judicial for each item you read. After students have responded to all ten, read them the correct answers:

1. President		1. Executive
2. Judge		2. Judicial
3. Courts		3. Judicial
4. Congress		4. Legislative
5. Governor		5. Executive
6. Senator		6. Legislative
7. House of Representatives		7. Legislative
8. Mayor		8. Executive
9. City Council		9. Legislative
10. State Legislature		10. Legislative

Class discussion (about 10 minutes)

- Ask the class: "Which branch of the government is the most important and why?"

Completing today's assignment (about 10 minutes)

- Have each student write a short paragraph on the same piece of paper he or she has been using. Start with the topic sentence: "All three branches of the government do important things."

After each student finishes today's work, it is to be handed in to you, and the student is to start the work that is due at the beginning of the period tomorrow.

- Have each student label three columns on a new sheet of paper and list five things for each column that would happen if each branch did not exist.

  No Legislative Branch   **No Executive Branch**   **No Judicial Branch**

Grade 9, Social Studies
American Government, Lesson Plan 3

Preparing to work (about 5 minutes)

- Take roll if required to do so.
- Have each student take out a sheet of paper and place the usual classroom heading on it—name, and so on.
- Have students write the topic for the day at the top of their papers: "Political Parties in the United States."

Understanding and applying basic facts (about 20 minutes)

- Have students *write* the following facts on their papers while you make any relevant comments you choose to make that will clarify the facts:

  A. The U.S. Constitution does not say that there will be political parties, but it does say that people will have freedom of speech and assembly.

  B. Being able to get together and express opinions led to people forming political parties.

  C. Since the time of the Civil War (1861–1865) the two major parties have been the Democrats and the Republicans.

  D. Other political parties are free to form, but no minor party has replaced a major party since the Republicans replaced the Whigs about the time of the Civil War.

- Have students number from 1 to 10 on their papers and guess by *writing* Democrat or Republican for each president you name. After students have responded to all ten, read them the correct answers:

1. George Walker Bush (2001–)		1.	Republican
2. Bill Clinton (1993–2001)		2.	Democrat
3. George Herbert Walker Bush (1989–1993)		3.	Republican
4. Ronald Reagan (1981–1989)		4.	Republican
5. Jimmy Carter (1977–1981)		5.	Democrat
6. Gerald Ford (1974–1977)		6.	Republican
7. Richard Nixon (1969–1974)		7.	Republican
8. Lyndon B. Johnson (1963–1969)		8.	Democrat
9. John F. Kennedy (1961–1963)		9.	Democrat
10. Dwight D. Eisenhower (1953–1961)		10.	Republican

Class discussion (about 10 minutes)

- Ask the class: "Could it ever happen that there would only be just one political party in the United States, and if so, what would it mean?"

Completing today's assignment (about 10 minutes)

- Have each student write a short paragraph on the same piece of paper he or she has been using. Start with the topic sentence: "Political parties are very important in the United States."

After each student finishes today's work, it is to be handed in to you, and the student is to start the work that is due at the beginning of the period tomorrow.

- Have each student list on a new sheet of paper ten important things political parties do. An example is given:

  1. Select candidates

Grade 10, Social Studies
World History, Lesson Plan 1

Preparing to work (about 5 minutes)

- Take roll if required to do so.
- Have each student take out a sheet of paper and place the usual classroom heading on it—name, and so on.
- Have students write the topic for the day at the top of their papers: "Ancient Civilizations."

Understanding and applying basic facts (about 20 minutes)

- Have students *write* the following facts on their papers while you make any relevant comments you choose to make that will clarify the facts:

    A. Three important ancient civilizations were the Egyptian, Greek, and Roman.

    B. By about 3500 B.C. the Egyptians were writing and doing things we label as "civilization."

    C. Greek city-states were developing by 800 B.C. Under the leadership of Pericles from 461 B.C. to 429 B.C., Athens enjoyed a "Golden Age."

    D. Ancient Rome lasted about a thousand years (roughly 509 B.C. to A.D. 476). Rome was a republic for a long time and then became a dictatorship under emperors for a long time.

- Have students number from 1 to 10 on their papers and guess by *writing* Egypt, Greece, or Rome for each item you read. After students have responded to all ten, read the correct answers:

    1. Pyramids
    2. Great roads
    3. Idea of democracy
    4. Parthenon
    5. Legions
    6. Colosseum
    7. Cement (invented it)
    8. Began drama (plays)
    9. Invented decimal system
    10. Hieroglyphics

    1. Egypt
    2. Rome
    3. Greece
    4. Greece
    5. Rome
    6. Rome
    7. Rome
    8. Greece
    9. Egypt
    10. Egypt

Class discussion (about 10 minutes)

- Ask the class: "What are some of the things in our modern world that we can trace back to the Egyptians, Greeks, and Romans?"

Completing today's assignment (about 10 minutes)

- Have each student write a short paragraph on the same piece of paper he or she has been using. Start with the topic sentence: "Our modern world owes much to ancient civilizations."

After each student finishes today's work, it is to be handed in to you, and the student is to start the work that is due at the beginning of the period tomorrow.

- Have each student label three columns on a new sheet of paper and list five things he or she thinks might fit each column. An example is given:

Ancient Egypt	**Ancient Greece**	**Ancient Rome**
1. Built pyramids	1. Started democracy	1. Powerful conquerors

Grade 10, Social Studies
World History, Lesson Plan 2

Preparing to work (about 5 minutes)

- Take roll if required to do so.
- Have each student take out a sheet of paper and place the usual classroom heading on it—name, and so on.
- Have students write the topic for the day at the top of their papers: "The Middle Ages in Europe."

Understanding and applying basic facts (about 20 minutes)

- Have students *write* the following facts on their papers while you make any relevant comments you choose to make that will clarify the facts:
  - A. After the fall of the Roman Empire, Europe entered a period of history known as the "Middle Ages."
  - B. The Middle Ages (Medieval) lasted roughly from A.D. 500 to A.D. 1500, with the "Renaissance" of the 1300s and 1400s signaling the end of the Middle Ages.
  - C. During the Middle Ages, the Roman Catholic Church (church) had great influence on kings (state) and on feudalism (economic system).
  - D. A code of conduct called "chivalry" defined how knights were to behave in battle and toward others.
- Have students number from 1 to 10 on their papers and guess by *writing* Church, State, or Feudalism for each item you read. After students have responded to all ten, read the correct answers:

1. Gothic architecture
2. Manor
3. St. Thomas Aquinas
4. Lord and serf
5. Pope Gregory VII
6. King Henry II
7. Vassal
8. Magna Carta
9. Parliament
10. Monastery

1. Church
2. Feudalism
3. Church
4. Feudalism
5. Church
6. State
7. Feudalism
8. State
9. State
10. Church

Class discussion (about 10 minutes)

• Ask the class: "What were the Crusades, and why were they undertaken?"

Completing today's assignment (about 10 minutes)

• Have each student write a short paragraph on the same piece of paper he or she has been using. Start with the topic sentence: "Chivalry, which in theory placed women on a pedestal as objects for knights to cherish and protect, might not work today."

After each student finishes today's work, it is to be handed in to you, and the student is to start the work that is due at the beginning of the period tomorrow.

• Have each student label three columns on a new sheet of paper and list five things he or she thinks might fit each column. An example is given:

Church	*State*	*Feudalism*
1. Popes	1. Kings	1. Manors

Grade 10, Social Studies
World History, Lesson Plan 3

Preparing to work (about 5 minutes)

• Take roll if required to do so.
• Have each student take out a sheet of paper and place the usual classroom heading on it—name, and so on.
• Have students write the topic for the day at the top of their papers: "Renaissance, Reformation, and Revolution."

Understanding and applying basic facts (about 20 minutes)

- Have students *write* the following facts on their papers while you make any relevant comments you choose to make that will clarify the facts:

    A. The transformation of the Middle Ages to the more modern world was brought about, in part, by the Renaissance, the Reformation, and revolutions.

    B. The Renaissance (roughly 1350–1600) was a period of great creativity in ideas and the arts.

    C. The Reformation (1500s) was an attempt to reform (change) the Roman Catholic Church that resulted in splitting the church into two parts, Catholic and Protestant.

    D. After the Middle Ages, many important revolutions happened.

- Have students number from 1 to 10 on their papers and guess by *writing* Renaissance, Reformation, or Revolution for each item you read. After students have responded to all ten, read the correct answers:

    1. Martin Luther   1. Reformation
    2. Mona Lisa   2. Renaissance
    3. Michelangelo   3. Renaissance
    4. American   4. Revolution
    5. French   5. Revolution
    6. Scientific   6. Revolution
    7. Industrial   7. Revolution
    8. Henry VIII's divorce   8. Reformation
    9. Indulgences   9. Reformation
    10. Sistine Chapel ceiling 10. Renaissance

Class discussion (about 10 minutes)

- Ask the class: "Are Catholics and Protestants different, or are they pretty much the same?"

Completing today's assignment (about 10 minutes)

- Have each student write a short paragraph on the same piece of paper he or she has been using. Start with the topic sentence: "The Renaissance and the Reformation brought about changes."

After each student finishes today's work, it is to be handed in to you, and the student is to start the work that is due at the beginning of the period tomorrow.

- Have each student label three columns on a new sheet of paper and list five things he or she thinks might fit each column. An example is given:

Renaissance	*Reformation*	*Revolution*
1. Great paintings	1. Lutherans	1. American

Grade 11, Social Studies
American History, Lesson Plan 1

Preparing to work (about 5 minutes)

- Take roll if required to do so.
- Have each student take out a sheet of paper and place the usual classroom heading on it—name, and so on.
- Have students write the topic for the day at the top of their papers: "The Revolutionary War."

Understanding and applying basic facts (about 20 minutes)

- Have students *write* the following facts on their papers while you make any relevant comments you choose to make that will clarify the facts:
    A. The United States became an independent country by fighting the British in the Revolutionary War (1775–1783).
    B. The first battle between American and British troops took place in 1775, even before the Declaration of Independence was signed in 1776.
    C. The Battle of Saratoga was a turning point in the war, when American forces defeated a British invasion from Canada in 1777.
    D. The British were defeated at Yorktown in 1781, but a peace treaty was not signed until 1783.
- Have students number from 1 to 10 on their papers and guess by *writing* British or American for each item you read. After students have responded to all ten, read the correct answers:

    1. Minutemen   1. American
    2. General Cornwallis   2. British
    3. General Burgoyne   3. British
    4. General Gates   4. American
    5. Continental Congress   5. American
    6. King George III   6. British
    7. French Alliance   7. American
    8. General Washington   8. American
    9. Parliament   9. British
    10. "Common Sense"   10. American

Class discussion (about 10 minutes)

- Ask the class: "Why were the Americans able to defeat the British when it is estimated that only about a third of the Americans supported the war, while a third remained loyal to the British, and the other third was undecided?"

Completing today's assignment (about 10 minutes)

- Have each student write a short paragraph on the same piece of paper he or she has been using. Start with the topic sentence: "A victory for the colonists in their revolt against England was not likely."

After each student finishes today's work, it is to be handed in to you, and the student is to start the work that is due at the beginning of the period tomorrow.

- Have each student label three columns on a new sheet of paper and list five things he or she thinks might fit each column. An example is given:

Rebel	*Loyalist*	*Undecided*
1. Wanted independence	1. Loyal to the King	1. Playing it safe

Grade 11, Social Studies
American History, Lesson Plan 2

Preparing to work (about 5 minutes)

- Take roll if required to do so.
- Have each student take out a sheet of paper and place the usual classroom heading on it—name, and so on.
- Have students write the topic for the day at the top of their papers: "Nineteenth-Century Wars."

Understanding and applying basic facts (about 20 minutes)

- Have students *write* the following facts on their papers while you make any relevant comments you choose to make that will clarify the facts:
    - A. The War of 1812 (1812–1814) resulted in the British getting out of American territory and leaving U.S. ships alone.
    - B. The Mexican War (1846–1848) settled a border dispute and acquired the Southwest for the United States.
    - C. The Civil War (1861–1865) preserved the United States and ended slavery.
    - D. The Spanish-American War (1898) ejected Spain from Cuba and gave the United States the Philippines, Puerto Rico, and Guam.
- Have students number from 1 to 10 on their papers and guess which war by *writing* War of 1812, Mexican War, Civil War, or Spanish-American War for each item you read. After students have responded to all ten, read the correct answers:

1. Rio Grande	1. Mexican War
2. Battleship *Maine*	2. Spanish-American War
3. Colonel Theodore Roosevelt	3. Spanish-American War

4. Gettysburg	4. Civil War
5. Burned Washington, D.C.	5. War of 1812
6. "The Star-Spangled Banner"	6. War of 1812
7. General Ulysses S. Grant	7. Civil War
8. Captured Mexico City	8. Mexican War
9. General Winfield Scott	9. Mexican War
10. Emancipation Proclamation	10. Civil War

Class discussion (about 10 minutes)

- Ask the class: "How would the United States be different today if it had lost any of these wars?"

Completing today's assignment (about 10 minutes)

- Have each student write a short paragraph on the same piece of paper he or she has been using. Start with the topic sentence: "The wars the United States fought in the nineteenth century were fought for various reasons."

After each student finishes today's work, it is to be handed in to you, and the student is to start the work that is due at the beginning of the period tomorrow.

- Have each student label four columns on a new sheet of paper and list five things he or she thinks might fit each column. An example is given:

War of 1812 (1812–1814)	*Mexican War (1846–1848)*	*Civil War (1861–1865)*	*Spanish-American War (1898)*
1. Burned Washington, D.C.	1. Southwest United States	1. Robert E. Lee	1. Guam

Grade 11, Social Studies
American History, Lesson Plan 3

Preparing to work (about 5 minutes)

- Take roll if required to do so.
- Have each student take out a sheet of paper and place the usual classroom heading on it—name, and so on.
- Have students write the topic for the day at the top of their papers: "Twentieth-Century Wars."

Understanding and applying basic facts (about 20 minutes)

- Have students *write* the following facts on their papers while you make any relevant comments you choose to make that will clarify the facts:

A. World War I (1914–1918): The United States fought in the war from 1917 to 1918. Our primary enemy was Germany.

B. World War II (1939–1945): The United States fought in the war from 1941 to 1945. Our primary enemies were Germany, Japan, and Italy for a while.

C. Korea (1950–1953) and Vietnam (1945–1975 for Vietnamese) (1962–1973 for Americans): The United States fought in both of these wars to try to keep a communist North from taking over a non-communist South.

D. Desert Storm (Gulf I) (1991): The war was fought to eject Iraq from Kuwait.

- Have students number from 1 to 10 on their papers and guess which war by *writing* WWI, WWII, Korea, Vietnam, or Gulf I for each item you read. After students have responded to all ten, read the correct answers:

1. Japan attacked China	1.	WWII
2. Iraq attacked Kuwait	2.	Gulf I
3. North Korea attacked South Korea	3.	Korea
4. North Vietnam waged war on South Vietnam	4.	Vietnam
5. Germany sunk the *Lusitania*	5.	WWI
6. D-Day	6.	WWII
7. Kuwait City	7.	Gulf I
8. Tet	8.	Vietnam
9. Inchon	9.	Korea
10. Meuse-Argonne Offensive	10.	WWI

Class discussion (about 10 minutes)

- Ask the class: "Why were the wars that the United States fought in the twentieth century not fought on U.S. soil?"

Completing today's assignment (about 10 minutes)

- Have each student write a short paragraph on the same piece of paper he or she has been using. Start with the topic sentence: "The wars that the United States fought in the twentieth century were similar in some ways, but different in other ways."

After each student finishes today's work, it is to be handed in to you, and the student is to start the work that is due at the beginning of the period tomorrow.

- Have each student label five columns on a new sheet of paper and list five things he or she thinks might fit each column. An example is given:

WWI	*WWII*	*Korea*	*Vietnam*	*Gulf I*
1. <u>Lusitania</u>	1. D-Day	1. Inchon	1. Tet	1. Kuwait attacked

Grade 12, Social Studies
Economics, Lesson Plan 1

Preparing to work (about 5 minutes)

- Take roll if required to do so.
- Have each student take out a sheet of paper and place the usual classroom heading on it—name, and so on.
- Have students write the topic for the day at the top of their papers: "Economic Systems."

Understanding and applying basic facts (about 20 minutes)

- Have students *write* the following facts on their papers while you make any relevant comments you choose to make that will clarify the facts:

  A. Economics is about how goods are produced, distributed, and consumed. Although countries do not have all of one economic system or another, countries in the modern world, generally, have capitalism, socialism, or communism.

  B. Capitalism, generally, has private ownership.

  C. Socialism, generally, has a large combination of both private ownership and government ownership.

  D. Communism, generally, has no private ownership.

- Have students number from 1 to 10 on their papers and guess by *writing* Capitalism, Socialism, or Communism for each item you read. After students have responded to all ten, read the correct answers:

  1. Stockholders
  2. Adam Smith
  3. Karl Marx
  4. Sweden
  5. China
  6. Canada's National Health Care
  7. Coca-Cola
  8. Government-owned railroad, but private taxis
  9. Private ownership of big and small businesses
  10. Soviet Union before it broke into individual nations

  1. Capitalism
  2. Capitalism
  3. Communism
  4. Socialism
  5. Communism
  6. Socialism
  7. Capitalism
  8. Socialism
  9. Capitalism
  10. Communism

Class discussion (about 10 minutes)

- Say to the class: "The United States is a very capitalistic country, but has some elements of socialism. What are the elements of socialism, and why does the United States have them?"

Completing today's assignment (about 10 minutes)

- Have each student write a short paragraph on the same piece of paper he or she has been using. Start with the topic sentence: "Capitalism and communism are very different from each other."

After each student finishes today's work, it is to be handed in to you, and the student is to start the work that is due at the beginning of the period tomorrow.

- Have each student label three columns on a new sheet of paper and list five things he or she thinks might fit each column. An example is given:

Capitalism	***Socialism***	***Communism***
1. Lots of private ownership	1. Government and private ownership	1. Very little private ownership

Grade 12, Social Studies
Economics, Lesson Plan 2

Preparing to work (about 5 minutes)

- Take roll if required to do so.
- Have each student take out a sheet of paper and place the usual classroom heading on it—name, and so on.
- Have students write the topic for the day at the top of their papers: "The U.S. Economy."

Understanding and applying basic facts (about 20 minutes)

- Have students *write* the following facts on their papers while you make any relevant comments you choose to make that will clarify the facts:
    A. The U.S. economy operates within a framework of capitalism (private ownership) and has three key elements: freedom of choice, competition, and profit.
    B. Freedom of choice in the economic sense is the right to operate whatever lawful business you choose to operate and the freedom to choose any lawful occupation.
    C. Competition among businesses means that some businesses will succeed and some businesses will fail.
    D. Profit motivates people to own and operate businesses.

- Have students number from 1 to 10 on their papers and guess by *writing* Choice, Competition, or Profit for each item you read. After students have responded to all ten, read the correct answers:

1.	Red Apple Sale	1.	Competition
2.	Become a lion tamer	2.	Choice
3.	Dividend	3.	Profit
4.	Newspaper advertisement	4.	Competition
5.	Going-out-of-business sale	5.	Competition
6.	Reward for taking risks	6.	Profit
7.	Money to invest	7.	Profit
8.	Open a laundromat	8.	Choice
9.	Buy Disney stock instead of Pepsi stock	9.	Choice
10.	Boycott a concert	10.	Choice

Class discussion (about 10 minutes)

- Ask the class: "What limits on freedom are there in the U.S. economy, and should there be limits?"

Completing today's assignment (about 10 minutes)

- Have each student write a short paragraph on the same piece of paper he or she has been using. Start with the topic sentence: "Freedom to choose in an economic sense affects my life in many ways."

After each student finishes today's work, it is to be handed in to you, and the student is to start the work that is due at the beginning of the period tomorrow.

- Have each student label three columns on a new sheet of paper and list five things he or she thinks might fit each column. An example is given:

Choice	*Competition*	*Profit*
1. Open a business	1. Advertise	1. Rewards effort

Grade 12, Social Studies
Economics, Lesson Plan 3

Preparing to work (about 5 minutes)

- Take roll if required to do so.
- Have each student take out a sheet of paper and place the usual classroom heading on it—name, and so on.
- Have students write the topic for the day at the top of their papers: "Demand, Supply, Price."

Understanding and applying basic facts (about 20 minutes)

- Have students *write* the following facts on their papers while you make any relevant comments you choose to make that will clarify the facts:

    A. In a capitalistic economy, like the United States has, demand, supply, and price are closely related and greatly influence each other.

    B. In general, increasing demand for a product causes a higher price for the product.

    C. In general, increasing supply of a product causes a lower price for the product.

    D. In general, lowering the price of a product increases the demand for the product.

- Have students number from 1 to 10 on their papers and guess by *writing* the likely first result in the form of "increase" or "lower" in regard to demand, supply, or price for each item you read. After students have responded to all ten, read the correct answers:

    1. Lower price
    2. Increase demand
    3. Lower supply
    4. Lower demand
    5. Increase price
    6. Increase supply
    7. Increase demand and lower supply
    8. Lower demand and increase supply
    9. Increase supply and lower price
    10. Lower supply and increase price

    1. Increase demand
    2. Increase price
    3. Increase price
    4. Lower price
    5. Lower demand
    6. Lower price
    7. Increase price
    8. Lower price
    9. Increase demand
    10. Lower demand

Class discussion (about 10 minutes)

- Ask the class: "What things other than supply and demand influence price?"

Completing today's assignment (about 10 minutes)

- Have each student write a short paragraph on the same piece of paper he or she has been using. Start with the topic sentence: "Consumers in the United States are very important in determining demand, supply, and price."

After each student finishes today's work, it is to be handed in to you, and the student is to start the work that is due at the beginning of the period tomorrow.

- Have each student label three columns on a new sheet of paper and list five things he or she thinks might fit each column. An example is given:

Demand	**Supply**	**Price**
1. Willingness to purchase product	1. Availability of product	1. Cost of product

Epilogue

I have purposely not suggested a so-called "bag of tricks." Although some substitutes may find puzzles, games, mind exercises, and other throw-in-quick activities valuable to fill spare moments or "downtime," they are not part of the curriculum. In my opinion, anything that takes away from following the curriculum and staying on target with prescribed learning is detrimental.

A "bag of tricks" may also foster the attitude that if the substitute does not like the prescribed lesson plan, the substitute can hurry through it and get to a "fun" activity of his or her choosing. Why should a substitute struggle with tough learning that kids moan and groan over when the easy way out is to pull out the "bag of tricks"? The answer is because that is the substitute's job, just as it is the regular teacher's job, to stay focused on the curriculum and to make every minute count, whether the task is easy or difficult.

"A bag of tricks" attitude on the part of the regular teacher can be as bad as a "bag of tricks" attitude on the part of the substitute. It is the regular teacher's responsibility to leave in place a viable and valuable lesson plan for the substitute to follow. "Oh well, the substitute will have something to throw in if this doesn't work out" is a sloppy way to construct a lesson plan that is supposed to keep the kids going in the curriculum where they should go.

As Ben Franklin said, "Waste not, want not." In my opinion, learning time is too valuable to waste on fill-in activities that don't follow the curriculum.

Of course, as always, I can stand corrected. If a "bag of tricks" increases a substitute's sense of security and it can be used effectively and enhances classroom learning, by all means use it. For me, and maybe not you, I have found a "bag of tricks" more of a detriment to learning than a help.

It is my hope that the suggestions made in this book are of value to you. Whether you are a substitute teacher or a regular teacher, I wish you every success in the noble purpose of educating our children.

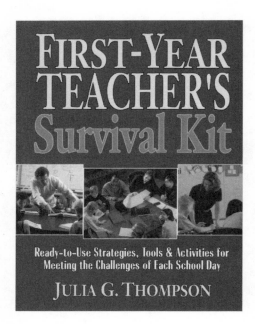

First-Year Teacher's Survival Kit

Ready-to-Use Strategies, Tools & Activities for Meeting the Challenges of Each School Day

Julia G. Thompson

Cloth   ISBN: 0-13-061644-3

www.josseybass.com

Begin the school year with confidence, set up your classroom routines to save time and work, get students motivated and ready to learn, and avoid personal burnout with the practical advice in the *First-Year Teacher's Survival Kit*. For easy use, this comprehensive resource is organized into 16 sections covering everything from motivation, lesson planning and classroom management, to behavior problems, meeting each student's needs, and building strong professional relationships with students, staff, and parents.

The down-to-earth suggestions in this book will provide good counsel through many years of teaching and will help make your job easier and more fulfilling.

Here's what's inside:

- Your New Vocation
- Develop Your Professional Expertise
- Begin the School Year with Confidence
- Become a Valuable Team Player
- Connect with Your Students
- Design Effective Instruction
- Deliver Effective Instruction
- Evaluate Your Students' Progress

- Motivate Your Students to Succeed
- Help Your Students Become Successful Learners
- Make the Most of Your Instructional Time
- Classroom Management Through Early Intervention
- Handle Behavior Problems Effectively
- Solutions for Some Widespread Problems
- The Diverse Classroom
- Stress Management for Educators

Julia G. Thompson (B.A., Virginia Polytechnic Institute and State University) has taught various secondary courses in the public schools of Arizona, North Carolina, and Virginia for over 20 years, including geography, reading, home economics, math, history, special education, and graduate equivalency preparation. She is currently teaching English at Churchland High School in Portsmouth, Virginia.